What You See...
Is What You Get

Portia A. Jones

BALBOA.PRESS
A DIVISION OF HAY HOUSE

Balboa Press books may be ordered through booksellers or by contacting:

Balboa Press
A Division of Hay House
1663 Liberty Drive
Bloomington, IN 47403
www.balboapress.com
844-682-1282

Because of the dynamic nature of the Internet, any web addresses or links contained in this book may have changed since publication and may no longer be valid. The views expressed in this work are solely those of the author and do not necessarily reflect the views of the publisher, and the publisher hereby disclaims any responsibility for them.

The author of this book does not dispense medical advice or prescribe the use of any technique as a form of treatment for physical, emotional, or medical problems without the advice of a physician, either directly or indirectly. The intent of the author is only to offer information of a general nature to help you in your quest for emotional and spiritual well-being. In the event you use any of the information in this book for yourself, which is your constitutional right, the author and the publisher assume no responsibility for your actions.

Scripture taken from the King James Version of the Bible.

Print information available on the last page.

ISBN: 979-8-7652-3902-5 (sc)
ISBN: 979-8-7652-3904-9 (hc)
ISBN: 979-8-7652-3903-2 (e)

Library of Congress Control Number: 2023902510

Balboa Press rev. date: 03/23/2023

DEDICATION

This book is dedicated to my parents, McKenly and Elease Bacon, both of whom are deceased. We miss them dearly.

ACKNOWLEDGEMENT

First of all, I want to give thanks to my Creator, my Maintainer, and my Sustainer—that divine presence that I call God. I give thanks for my life, my family, my friends, my health, and for all the good with which I have been blessed.

I want to acknowledge and give thanks to all those who have so often said to me after a speaking engagement or after a private conversation, "Girl, you need to write a book!" I won't venture to specifically name these wonderful angels in my life because I don't want to omit any deserving one of you, but you know who you are, and I recognize that I am blessed for having you in my life and on my side. So please know that I appreciate all of you. Please accept my gratitude for your belief in me.

Another round of applause for those of you at Balboa Publishing who have displayed so much patience and understanding from the beginning to the end of this endeavor. Thank you all!

Peace, love, and blessings!

CONTENTS

INTRODUCTION

This is a book that has been on my mind for more than twenty years! Specifically, the title. For all those years, I told myself and anyone who would listen to me that there was at least one book within me that was waiting to be written. Now, however, there may be others that are waiting to press out as well.

The title of this book comes from the comedian Flip Wilson, who had a variety television program called *The Flip Wilson Show* from 1970 through 1974 on NBC TV. In one of his comedy skits, he played a female character named Geraldine. Now, Geraldine was a hair slinging, hip switching sister who didn't put up with anyone's negative attitude toward her—especially from men. She was truly a women's liberator. She was independent and extremely vocal about her thoughts and feelings on any given topic. When a man commented about her personality or looks, she would stand tall, flip her wig, place her hands on her hips, and sharply retort, "What you see is what you get!" Her message was very clear.

Geraldine was referring to physical seeing, but in this book, I will use the term "seeing" as our ability to understand life on a deeper level. Sometimes after reading what people have written or listening to what they have said, we may feel some uncertainty or confusion about the message they were trying to convey to us. However, after the matter has been cleared up, we might say, "Oh, I see what you are saying!" This means we now understand what was previously unclear to us. Therefore, it is my intent to use Geraldine's statement "What you see is what you get" as a way to assist those who are seeking to enhance their awareness of a greater understanding of their relationship with each other and with the universe. And with this heightened awareness, I believe we all will come to understand that it is our perceptions that become our realities. My intention in writing this book is to help those who are seeking a deeper understanding of life's questions to no longer accept the surface or obvious answers to some of life's uncertainties or mysteries and to begin to take back their own power and no longer allow themselves to be manipulated like a ship without an anchor on a constant ocean storm.

Metaphysically, this is known as our consciousness. Our thoughts and feelings about what we experience becomes our reality; that is, what I accept, understand, and ultimately believe is actually the essence of my belief system. In other words, what we perceive becomes our reality regardless of what actually occurs. Therefore, our life experiences are based on what we perceive as our truth and not necessarily what happens. Our lives show up based on what we "see," and that determines how we react or respond to all of the situations, circumstances, and conditions that daily confront us.

This is the essence of my book. So, based on my own numerous life experiences, stories of those whom I have had the opportunities to counsel through lesson sermons, workshops, and in those times of just sharing our life stories with each other, I know that our lives are a culmination of ...

"What You See... Is What You Get!"

Chapter 1

IN THE BEGINNING

To those of you who are already familiar with the metaphysical philosophy, be it formal or informal, and to those who are unfamiliar with this field of study and yet are open and receptive to simply listening to what I've got to say, I say thank you. I appreciate you, and I am grateful for your willingness to being open to "seeing" my perspective on life. I make no effort to convince anyone, and just as importantly, I do not apologize for the way I "see" and have been living my life according to this perspective.

Thank you so very much for taking this journey with me, which I believe will be enlightening as well as enjoyable! So let's begin this trek of realizing that, in life …

"What You See... Is What You Get!"

Chapter 2

AND A CHILD SHALL LEAD THEM

As a child, I was raised in the Baptist religion. At that time, children were not allowed to ask questions of adults, especially not ones concerning religion or God. We just had to listen to our parents, ministers, teachers, or any adult for that matter and accept whatever was said to us. However, as a kid with an inquiring mind, I always had questions that I wanted answers to. Of course, there was no way to make these inquiries. Many of my questions had to do with how the adults—especially those who attended church every Sunday—felt about and related to God. It seemed to me that God was mostly talked about on Sundays or when things weren't going well. However, based on my observations of the adults around me, my child's mind concluded that faith in God meant that, when you were in difficult situations, you prayed to God. Those were the times when adults would ask for help, and so they then expected God to show up at that time of need.

That little girl noticed that little attention was given to God except on Sundays or during times of difficulty. Those teachers (all the adults around me) expected answers from God, and if they were churchgoing folks, they would receive answers, yet it was not always the ones they were hoping for. And those who felt that they weren't "good" enough would bargain with God by promising a change of heart and mind, promising to attend church services more frequently, or making some other promises in order to get their wishes fulfilled.

That little girl wanted to ask so many questions about this interaction. Who was God and where was he? Why were these adults bothering to pray to God for an answer to their problems? Did they really believe that they would receive answers? How did they know that God would answer their prayers? How did they know that God would even hear their prayers, especially since they had admitted that they had not been in touch with God in a very long time? Did God respond only to those who were good? These were just a few of the questions that that little girl wanted answers to.

I later learned that these people had what is called "blind faith" in God; that is, they didn't recognize that they were using spiritual principles that could not or would not hold anything against them regardless of what they had done previously. They didn't know that, because they were acknowledging the presence and power of God at that particular moment, and they truly believed that their prayers would be answered as long as their prayers were in alignment with the spiritual principles, they would, indeed, receive an answer to their prayers.

But there was another aspect on which the little girl pondered as well. She constantly heard the adults complaining about their problems. In the child's mind, according to ministers' sermons, all you had to do to solve your problems was to simply ask God for whatever it was you wanted. So, here again, she wanted to ask those adults, "Well, why don't you just pray to God to solve this problem?" As I look back at this child with the inquiring mind, I wonder about those teachers who constantly complained. Did they not have enough faith to turn to God, acknowledge God's presence and power, and pray for the resolution of the problems about which they were worrying? As I look back, I wonder if they were not aware of this truth that ...

"What You See... Is What You Get!"

Chapter 3

WHAT IS THIS THING CALLED FAITH?

I guess, based on my childhood experiences, faith just didn't make sense to me. Of course, no one explained faith to me, and even after joining the community of metaphysicians and doing extensive reading, I still didn't have a solid understanding of what faith was all about. This issue of faith just didn't make a whole lot of sense to me. So, as a young adult, I decided to remove myself from the Baptist church. And after trying many other religions, I ultimately just gave up on God. I decided that people who said they believed in God were not consistent; they couldn't provide satisfactory answers to my many questions about their relationship with God.

I decided to live my life without believing in any religion and without any consideration of God. Claiming that God was involved in our daily life experiences just didn't make sense to me. However, my religious roots were too deep to deny the existence of God. I was afraid that if I lived my life denying the existence of a God, I would end up in eternal hell. So, like the adults that the little girl had observed, I sort of made a bargain with God and called myself an agnostic. I rationalized that, in this way, at the time of my passing, I would have some bargaining room with God. I decided that since I had not totally denied the existence of God—I had only questioned God's existence—I should be given some leeway for consideration to enter heaven.

In 1979, when I first joined a Unity Church in Atlanta and began my formal education in metaphysical studies, I came across a book entitled *"Magic of Faith" by Dr. Joseph Murphy. At that time in my life,* I found both the statements about faith and this or any other book referring to this topic to be very challenging and still wasn't making sense to me. I read the meaning of faith in the Bible. "Faith is the essence of things hoped for and the evidence of things not seen." Its meaning still boggled my mind. So ultimately, every time I read the word *faith*, I would end up with a question: "What?" And whenever I purchased a book, I would skip the chapters or pages on that topic. If a book had the word *faith as part of* its title, I would not purchase it.

Some of my greatest moments occur when I am reading about our relationship with that Universal Life Force and when I am trying to understand that relationship on a deeper plane rather than accepting a superficial view of our life struggles, our accomplishments, our desires, our failures, our hopes, and our dreams. For the first time in my life, I was learning about a God who wasn't a man in the sky who was busy keeping track of the numerous mistakes that might or might not keep me from entering the pearly gates of heaven. Ultimately, I came to understand that God is not a man in human form but an invisible presence, a tremendous force, power or being—a kind of energy or power that is omnipotent, omnipresent, and omniscient—and that this power is ever available to me even though I may not be able to see it with my physical eyes, touch it, or prove its existence in any way other than by believing it, acknowledging it, and accepting it as what I have come to know as the truth. At a much later time, I came to understand that faith is based on my willingness to rely on, depend on someone or something when I need help in accomplishing a specific goal or when I want to attain some specific good. That's my current understanding of what faith really is.

This presence is always available to us all at all times. Through this metaphysical perspective, I have come to learn that there are specific spiritual laws. Through my studies and constant practice, I have come to know that there is a power or a presence that is within me; this presence is an energy like electricity—but greater. This energy responds to everyone according to the way we think and feel. It's like using an iron. I can plug an iron into a socket and select the energy level from low to high. But if I don't bother to plug in the iron at all, then I can't have the advantage that a heated iron provides.

In the same way, our lives are impacted based on the level of our belief in ourselves and in that invisible presence. We can decide to plug in or not. We can further decide at what level we intend to use this energy. And this energy or power is ever responding to us. This is a basic law of that power that dwells within all of us. When the power of electricity became known to humankind, I am certain that many individuals were skeptical about it. But once we became familiar with it, we were more accepting of its use. In the same way, because they are not even aware of any spiritual laws regarding our thoughts and feelings, people may laugh at or even scorn the idea of them. Yet biblical scholars around the world verify that Jesus alluded to spiritual principles or laws throughout his ministry. But if you don't try it, you won't ever get to know how to use this power or presence. You will never learn its practicality, ease of use, and usefulness. When the ancient Greeks figured out that the world was not flat, many people, of course, laughed at the idea. When Galileo proclaimed that the sun did not revolve around the earth, but rather that the earth revolved around the sun, again, most did not believe him. And in fact, the Catholic Church had him declared a heretic and imprisoned him for many years. Yet these facts were ultimately proved to be true.

And for this reason, you may never experience the greater joy, peace, love, health, and wealth because of that spiritual law called

"What You See... Is What You Get!"

Chapter 4

THOUGHTS ARE THINGS

In the early 1900's, Dr. Ernest Holmes founded the metaphysical organization called Science of Mind, sometimes referred to as Religious Science (not to be confused with L. Ron Hubbard's Scientology). Dr. Holmes authored many books including one entitled *Thoughts Are Things*. I read this book several times some years ago, and as I look back now, I realize how little I really understood or was ready to accept this concept. Even though I didn't fully understand this concept, I began to notice that I'd had experiences in my own life that were, indeed, parallel to my thoughts, which is the concept that Holmes was trying to convey to his followers. So I began to be more attentive to my thoughts, my feelings, and my speech – which is termed my "consciousness".

In fact, there have been many renowned scientists (including Albert Einstein) who have verified that thoughts are a kind of energy. Webster defines energy as a conserved quantity that can be converted into form. Scientists have verified that energy cannot be created or destroyed. Energy just is. And many scientists and especially those scientists who specialize in the study of Quantum Physics) are now in alignment with this definition of God.

After discerning this kind of information about energy, I began to give even further consideration to the idea that thoughts are things and can possibly be converted into actual life experiences. After much research, study and practice, I became more confident about this teaching and philosophy. After becoming a teacher in the New York City public school system, I wanted my students to be as successful as they possibly could be, so I created an affirmation that I felt might ultimately reach their subjective minds and eventually impact on their studies and overall school behavior and, of course, their later lives. So I created an affirmation that my students recited every morning before their classes began. Initially this was done in my homeroom only; however, a very wonderful and supportive principal heard my students reciting this affirmation and asked if I would be willing to share it with the entire school population. This was done. So, all students, every day before their teachers picked them up from the auditorium, would recite the following: "**I have a powerful mind, and I use my mind to become a powerful student!**"

After retiring from the public school system, I made a visit to my old school two or three years later. Surprisingly enough the student body was still reciting this affirmation before beginning their regular day. Hopefully there were some whose minds were changed as this statement sank deeply into their subconscious minds.

"What You See... Is What You Get!"

Chapter 5

STEPPING UP

*T*his teaching has now become more than a theory or a philosophy to me. It has begun to impact on every aspect of my life. Thus becoming a teacher, a practitioner and minister was an ultimate choice because I wanted to assist others who have been searching in the same manner that I did for something greater than what many have felt and feel that "... there must be more to life than this." When I made the first decision to step up, I believed that at that time in my life, since my life was going so well, how could I be an effective teacher? I felt that I had not experienced those difficult times in life which I felt made a great teacher and influencer. I thought that those kinds of experiences were the "stuff of life" as I became a spiritual counselor and adviser. The universe took care of this! Within a matter of months, my life took a 180-degree turn. It seemed that someone or something had the power to turn my life upside down. That was the very first time I began to seriously watch my thoughts, feelings, and spoken words. Of course, I realize that this is a concept that many will have great difficulty in accepting. But it might be easier for them to agree that both thoughts and feelings are invisible—like the air—but nonetheless have some kind of value and some kind of power that does affect our lives. Also, there is a lot of research that has been done by the major universities in this country and in Europe on this matter, and this research supports this metaphysical perspective as well. I am finding that many physicians are joining us in our belief system as well.

Another way of looking at this concept that thoughts are things is that, when we plant orange seeds in the fertile soil, ultimately the seeds, with proper care, will burst forth from the earth as a young plant. That plant has all its components: roots, trunk, branches, leaves, flowers, and, ultimately, oranges! So, if we plant orange seeds in fertile soil and nurture them, eventually orange trees will show up. In the same way, seeds of thoughts are planted in the cosmic soil of the universe—that is our minds. Eventually, like the physical seeds, they will manifest as specific corresponding experiences in our lives. Many have come to realize that thoughts are simply actions that are about to be born, just as orange seeds will eventually spring up as orange trees.

I truly believe this to be true. Of course, this is not the case for every single thought that we may have, but it is for those thoughts that are persistently and consistently crossing our minds and thus have made an impression on the subconscious aspect of our minds. This is very much like making an impression on a lump of clay that has been pounded on. The replica of that impounded impression will eventually appear.

Even if we are not religiously inclined, as we ponder our lives and life in general, we will probably become aware that there is something behind those things that are visibly seen by the human eye. Let's consider this: All those things that we can physically see originally began with a single idea or thought. Unquestionably we all recognize that ideas are invisible. Look at the things around you. From clothespins to computers, everything began as a single idea. An inventor believes his or her invisible idea is viable and takes the essential steps to manifest the idea. We all have benefitted because these women and men believed in themselves and their ideas. These people took a single idea (thought) to physical form on the earthly plane for humankind's use and convenience. So this energy called thought is absolutely powerful for sure.

Many have now come to know that, if they can control their thoughts—that is, change those negative ones into healthy, life-giving ones—they become the masters of their own fates. When we come to recognize this truism, we have greater faith in ourselves and our abilities, and we have an enhanced confidence to operate successfully in the world about us. This may be due to a realization and an acceptance that there is an inner "something" within us that empowers us to handle our lives. We may acknowledge that this is the real power of which we are the owners. I believe that this acknowledgement causes us to be more confident and creative. It makes us kinder and more giving to others. It makes us less fearful and less angry. All of this is possible simply because we have learned that thoughts are things that can be turned into physical realities of good for ourselves and others as well. You can certainly test and prove this concept for yourself. You can decide upon a specific goal to achieve, such as a new career choice, better health, more positive relationships (it's an endless list!) and become "the captain of your own ship" (your life). This realization can be life changing, because ...

"What You See... Is What You Get!"

13

Chapter 6

WHAT SPIRITUAL LAWS?

A law is defined as a rule of conduct that is established and enforced by an authority. Laws are created so that all concerned will experience some form of order rather than chaos. There are many different kinds of laws. There are general mathematical laws and there are specific algebraic laws. If we are doing an algebraic problem, we know for certain that if we are familiar with the algebraic laws, we expect that we will always get the correct answer to the problem as will everyone else who knows these laws and every time. There are laws that pertain to music; laws that are concerned with driving an automobile; laws of marriage; laws concerning the education of our children and the list goes on and on. This is not only true for this country but is also true for nations throughout the world.

They are laws or principles of life by which all the citizens of the world should expect others to follow as we do. These laws help to create a sense of order not chaos. Like any of the other laws, these laws are not specific to any individual or group of individuals but they are impersonal in nature. If we follow these laws to the best of our ability we can anticipate a fairly trouble free life; one of health, reasonable wealth and companionship with family and friends.

The highest court in our nation is the Supreme Court, and the highest form of government is the federal government. And, of course, there is a document that is called the Constitution, which is the ruling document in our nation. Then each city and state has its own laws that must fit within the parameters of those highest authorities of our country. When we violate the established laws, we put ourselves in jeopardy of being penalized for our decision. Being ignorant of the federal, state, or local laws is not an acceptable excuse. Each adult is expected to know these laws and make every effort to follow them or be faced with the consequences. These laws are not personal; they are for our general use for the effective operation of each community. Without these laws, we would be living in absolute chaos.

When we mistreat our physical environment, we should only expect the resultant consequences; for example, depletion of the ozone layer, climatic changes, endangering of species, and so forth. If we want to become proficient in any profession or area of life, we must learn and follow those rules that are particular to that specific area of concern. If we are unaware of the principles of piano playing, we will never become successful in that profession because we are lacking in the appropriate knowledge. So, being ignorant of the principles is not an excuse for our failure to attain our goals. It is just a matter of not knowing or ignorance. Hence, it is up to each of us to become aware of the laws or principles that govern whatever area of our lives in which we want to succeed. Getting a wrong answer to an algebraic problem is not a punishment; it is simply the consequences of not applying the proper laws. And offering the excuse "I didn't know that rule" is not a justification for the incorrect response.

In the same manner, there are spiritual or universal laws as well. However, most people are unaware of these as spiritual laws. Here is one such universal law: What you sow, you must reap. Another way of saying this is, do unto others as you would have them do unto you. Of course, we all are aware of this mandate, but we may not have realized that it is a spiritual or universal law to which we all are obligated. If we don't, we will experience the consequences of our actions. And, of course, our behavior is preceded by our thoughts. (See the prior chapter, "Thoughts Are Things.")

Those of us who are religiously or spiritually inclined, when we don't understand why we may be having difficult or challenging moments in our lives, when we stop blaming others or even ourselves or some outside source, we may come to realize that maybe we have violated some life rule or law. So, in order to redirect what is happening in our lives, we may discover that we need to change our minds to make our lives operate more proficiently. You can sit quietly with yourself and ask, "What is it that I need to think or do in order to alter the events in my life?" Because until we change our thoughts and behavior, we will continue to get the same results. As a pianist, if I continue to strike the wrong key I will get a discordance in the music I am playing. I notice this discordance and make a decision to change my behavior. I study and practice to get the sound that I desire; thereafter finding the key that I should be striking to obtain the right sound. With my new knowledge and awareness, I now strike the correct key. I now am experiencing the music I want to hear.

It's the same message in spiritual law in terms of how we play the game of life. When my life shows up in a discordant manner, I can change my focus and proceed by changing the choices I make.

Actually all laws work in the same manner. If we violate these laws, we will experience the consequences of noncompliance. Being ignorant of the laws is never an excuse.

We are not being punished by someone or something, spiritual or otherwise. We are simply having the experiences of not adhering to these laws – both natural laws and spiritual laws. The beauty of errors is that they can be corrected if and when we choose to. Regardless of our age or any other consideration, we can elect to change our lives by changing our minds so that we can live more productive, healthy, creative, and joy-filled lives!

In our scriptures, we are told that there is one supreme being and that we should honor this divine entity and only that one. However, when we don't follow this spiritual law, we will get corresponding experiences in our lives. The spiritual laws may even be seen as laws of common sense. If we practice the rules and regulations of a specific sport or musical activity, we will get corresponding results due to our commitment and practice of these rules. If we are kind and generous to people, we will get similar responses from others. If we steal from others, ultimately this must be our experience as well. Some may call this karma— but, rather I see it as a law that shows that the seeds that we plant will ultimately come back to reflect our thoughts and feelings.

Some understand this as the law of cause and effect. Another way of viewing this is, "As within, so without." Remember my earlier example of planting orange seeds with the expectation of harvesting oranges? If we are hateful and resentful toward others, isn't it unrealistic to expect others to be loving toward us? Isn't this and other behaviors in our life activities the same? If we believe that money is evil, why would we expect to see an abundance of money flowing freely in our lives? As in the earlier examples of math and musical laws, we see that by understanding and accepting these and other spiritual laws, we can live more joy-filled, creative and successful lives.

I believe that the greatest spiritual law of all is that of believing in the presence and power of that one supreme entity—which I and many others throughout the world call,"God". Of course, it is known by so many other names, but personally, I believe that the name itself doesn't matter. What does matter is the realization and acceptance of this law called "oneness". If we believe that there is the existence of this one and another one (that is, two powers), then it seems logical that we must have experiences that reflect or correspond to this other entity as well. Doesn't that make common sense? Yet, when I observe nature, I see the operation of oneness. I don't see differences in the way every aspect of nature procreates and functions. This seems to apply also to mankind. There is only the sameness throughout. I don't see chaos; rather, I see order and similarities. What a wonderful experience it is to know that we can count on this sameness of all—throughout the world—oneness. I find that to be awesome, compelling, and so very comforting.

Another law is that even our health can be impacted in a positive or negative manner according to what we believe. This refers to the idea that thoughts are things. We cannot consistently have negative thoughts of disease and poor health on our minds and expect to experience good health and strength. If we believe that the natural process of maturing is only seen as a debilitating and lack of vitality experience, then how can we possibly expect to show youthful vitality and vigor in the future?

The great athletes that we admire so much use these laws regularly by believing in their own abilities, skills and talents. In this way they are practicing (nurturing their positive thoughts) to attain their goals. Without consideration of the principle of "...As within,—so without", their goals would not attained.

And those of us who have paid attention to the inevitability regarding natural and/or spiritual laws we are pretty much in charge of our successful and joy-filled lives and are not deceived into believing that other people and events in our lives have control over us.

I believe, though, that the foremost law can be found in Isaiah 44:6: "I am the first and I am the last, and apart from me there is no other God." In other words, there is only one Power and one Presence. Let's suppose that a person believes that there is another power like the devil. The t.v. character, Geraldine, used to declare, "The devil made me do it!" Now those who believe in that other power called the devil must have experiences in life that reflect the qualities of that belief system. The law of, "As within,...so without" is always in operation. Again, this is an impersonal law that does not punish us, but we are subject to the consequences according to our belief.

So, for sure I believe that, by accepting, understanding, and practicing these spiritual laws,

"What You See... Is What You Get!"

Chapter 7

THIS THING CALLED FAITH

As I continue to deepen my spiritual awareness, I have come to know that I had to understand and accept that it was essential for me to look at this thing called faith. As I researched, read, and studied about this topic, I prayed for guidance in understanding faith. It became clear to me that I—as well as all of us—have always demonstrated faith to some degree in something or someone. The difference is in what or whom we have placed our faith. Today when I speak to audiences, I remind them of this very true fact.

When I initially joined my very first metaphysical church, I would evade reading that paragraph, page, chapter, or even a book if the word "Faith" was used. Eventually, though, I was forced to conclude that this was a subject that I had to confront if I was serious about deepening my spiritual growth. I finally had to admit that, if there was some issue that made me uncomfortable, then it was one to which I had to sit down and give my attention. I needed to know what this thing called faith was all about. And so my journey to accomplish this task began.

Most children grow up having faith in their parents whom they expect to love them, provide for them, and protect them.

Some time ago, I had the opportunity to observe a very interesting and impressive scene that helped me to look at and better understand "faith". A father was trying to teach his son how to swim. As the child stood on the edge of the pool, he seemed to be deliberating on whether he was going to dive in or not. Maybe he wondered if he could trust his father to catch him if he needed help. He continued to hesitate. The father patiently continued to stretch out his arms toward his son and to encourage him to jump. He tried to reassure the child by saying, "Come on ... jump! I will catch you. I promise you will be okay." Finally the child excitedly dove into the arms of his loving father. With delightful squeals of joy, he was absolutely pleased with the outcome of his jump.

As I observed this scenario, I realized that what I had just witnessed was "faith" in action. I then thought that faith must be believing and trusting that someone or something will do what has been promised. When we are in trouble, we do not waiver in that belief. Therefore, our trust, our dependence upon this person or thing, causes us to respond to life in a very confident manner because we are assured that something or someone always has our back. We can depend on that person or thing. In other words, we have faith in this person or thing.

As I have mentioned, the Bible tells us that, "Faith is the substance of things hoped for and the evidence of things not seen." Now I don't know about you, but every time I read this, I would always close the Bible with a sense of query and wonderment. This definition of "Faith" gave me no clarity—no understanding at all. I just didn't "see" it. But I kept looking at those persons and things in which we all have faith. I realized that I had faith in my keys to my car and my front door. I had faith in the mechanism of the key and the lock, and I never had doubts about the operation of the mechanism. I have never questioned or even bothered to think about the mechanism involved in accomplishing this task. I simply assumed, believed, and expected that my keys would start the engine of my car and would open the front door of my home. And I am willing to say that most of us have the same experience. It then occurred to me that, although I didn't consciously think of it, this—too—is faith in action.

We all (hopefully) place our faith in our employers whom we trust to treat us in a certain manner, and we have faith they will compensate us for the work that we have been assigned to do and have accomplished. If they fail to meet either of these expectations, then we are surprised, hurt, annoyed, and unhappy. We lose faith in them (especially if that undesired behavior continues). Once that faith has been broken, the relationship is altered in some way. As an example, I worked for a company who failed to provide compensation to its employees at the appropriate time. So, unlike that child who trusted his father to catch him when he jumped into the water, I no longer trusted the company's ability to compensate me. Therefore, I severed my relationship with that company due to my lack of confidence in or faith in it.

What I discovered in my search for meaning was that I really didn't know God. I got it that God is invisible; that is, spirit. Yet, as I noted in some examples here, we readily place our faith in many instances of nature. We have faith in the process that, when we plant an orange seed, we will get an orange tree. We trust; we have faith in this process. That little boy knew his father, so it was easy for him to trust him and jump into his arms. How do we place our faith in or trust in someone or something that we don't know or can't see? Yet, we do trust nature.

I have concluded that there are two major obstacles that prevent us from placing our faith in God. The first one is that God—or spirit—is invisible. The second one is that most people don't know God and have not studied and practiced the way mathematicians and musicians are compelled to do to become proficient in their areas of interest. Even though many Christians say they have faith in God, they don't really. It seems they are more comfortable placing their faith in those things they can see or touch and with which they have had some past experiences. Often, we take the word of ministers and others because of what we believe they know or have had experiences with God. My mission then became to discover the qualities and attributes of God; that is, to get to really know God based on what I had discovered for myself. I didn't want to depend on others' experiences. Again, to extend my examples of a math student and musical student, I couldn't rely upon someone else's knowledge and skills. Those who do not practice will never acquire expertise, no matter the discipline.

What are the qualities of God? I was determined to discover them. I began this journey of inquiry for I really wanted to know God for myself. When I needed help, as the scriptures advised me, I must know God for myself—not from what others have told me. I knew that I had to travel that journey of discovery on my own. So, my seeking to know gave me an experience that I can tell everyone about, including my deeper recognition of faith in this invisible presence.

This is only one of a few other ife-threatening events in which my faith played a key role:

There was a light drizzle as three of my friends and I were leaving New Orleans headed for a Religious Science conference in Tennessee. Suddenly the car started to hydroplane. Since I had been trained by a professional driving instructor, I was confident that I could handle the situation. So I didn't panic. Instead, I used everything that I had learned to correct the swerving of the car. Despite all my efforts, I was unable to affect any change. The car continued to veer onto the median and then back onto the slippery highway. As the skidding continued I realized that I had absolutely no control over the vehicle as it proceeded to leave the highway and head downward towards a nearby cliff. At that moment, I understood that I had lost all control over this frightening situation – so my only alternative was to pray. The only words that came out of my mouth was in the form of a chant, "Jesus, Jesus, Jesus". I didn't stop this chant until I heard one of my girlfriends say to me, "Portia, we're all okay." When I looked up and around, they were already standing outside of the car. Only I was inside the car and still holding onto the steering wheel. The car had stopped and everyone survived without a scratch.

Since that time, I have experienced at least three other life-threatening situations, and in each case, I came to understand and accept that, in such difficult situations, if I would simply recognize the presence and power of God for my protection and guidance, all things would work out for my highest good. So now I have a portfolio of experiences in which I have absolute evidence that there is a rationale for having faith in this Invisible Presence which I call God or sometimes Spirit or Heavenly Father. I can affirm that, in every situation in which my life and the lives of others around me have been challenged, I always look to that Invisible Force to come to my rescue.

Admittedly though, I am not as vigilant in all of my normal everyday situations. I have not always remembered to look to God and rely upon this Presence to rescue me. Nevertheless my repertoire of past experiences and my awareness of the qualities and attributes of God have caused me to trust and—to place my faith in that Presence and Power that is at all times ready to solve my problems. Now this is what I truly believe, and I have made a commitment to myself to give more attention to this Invisible Presence and enhance my faith more and more each day.

Only through our personal experiences with God can we come to learn about the attributes of God, and only through these personal experiences will we learn to place our faith in this Force. We are told in Scriptures that we must "walk" (think and act) in faith. This greater understanding has proven to me that, when I get to know God—at least on some level—like the child at the pool, I can learn to trust and to have greater faith in God.

I now am more certain that ...

"What You See... Is What You Get!"

Chapter 8

THE POWER WITHIN

Too few of us believe that we are these powerful beings and that we can accomplish whatever we choose if we have the interest, the talent, and the commitment to persevere. We can also choose to be healthy, happy, productive, creative, joyful, and successful beings in all areas of our lives. Those who have achieved great successes— well-known athletes, entrepreneurs, artisans, entertainers—know this very well. However, some of them may erroneously feel that their successes were accomplished through their own personal power and abilities. I have come to realize that those who believe this, though, have not yet attained the qualities of peace of mind, love, joy, and comfort. They may believe that they have a personal power of their own that does not emanate from anything other than themselves. Those of this belief may attain the same goals as those who realize that their accomplishments have to do with their belief in something greater than themselves.

We are powerful beings. When we view ourselves solely as human beings, we are so limited. With this perspective, we are at the mercy of all external conditions, situations, and circumstances.

However, with an awareness of an inner power that is ever available to us and – within us, we are guided and protected by that Inner Force, which is always at our disposal. If we look at people like the late Stephen Hawking, who was an author, a theoretical physicist, and a cosmologist, we have to see that what I say must be true. Many people, though, may dismiss his life as an exception rather than the rule. When Hawking was in his twenties, he was diagnosed with a motor neuron disease, but he did not allow this disabling condition to prevent him from reaching his numerous goals. He even defied what scientists and doctors declared would be his life expectancy. So we can question what power enabled him to be so prolific and achieve so much with such a seemingly debilitating disease. Hawking knew that he did not, of himself, have the power to achieve so very much. So what power was it that enabled him to be so successful? And, of course, we can name so many other people who defied all the naysayers and are now in our history books due to their achievements and service to the world at large.

Too often we get caught up in the name of this Power that is within us, and the name is irrelevant. Most of us grew up not being fully aware of this power within us, which is also the creative force in the universe. Most traditional Christians continue to believe that this power is outside of themselves—rather than an inner "something" that is ever present and always available to us. So they continue going through the motions of acknowledging that –"something" -- because, basically, that is what they have been taught. They go to church every Sunday and say they believe in this Entity. Their belief is that, when they die, they will be rewarded in a place called heaven. I remember asking a family member after he had returned home from a two-hour church service, what was the minister's message? He replied that the minister spoke very well, but he couldn't remember the topic on which he had spoken. So many church goers are proud that they attend church services every Sunday or at least periodically, -- but they too often don't remember the message. So how can they learn more about this Invisible Entity if they are not familiar with the characteristics and nature of God? The reason for their attending church service is mostly due to a habit which they learned from childhood. Unfortunately it is not about learning about the true nature of this indwelling Presence and their relationship with It.

Over the years, I have discovered that this is not unusual for many who religiously attend church services. They are not even aware that they should have developed some sort of a relationship with that Entity. There's nothing wrong with going to church every Sunday, but it is my personal belief that, if you are not leaving with a sense of having learned something more about this Entity and your relationship with that Presence and how it might help you become a better person and spiritually aware, you are definitely missing out.

We must learn and accept that there is a power that is not only available to each and every one of us, but that this Power is within us where no one or nothing can take it away from us or even alter our relationship with It. With this realization, we can take advantage of this power, and we will, indeed, discover that, through our belief in and trust in this power, all of our legitimate desires are possible.

If you have an inquiring mind very much like mine, you might look around at the physical world (nature) and observe the wonders that we usually take for granted. For example, did you ever wonder about our complex bodies and how they function without any conscious instructions from us? As human beings, we do not have the power within ourselves to heal a sickness or to maintain and sustain the extraordinary complexity of our bodies.

Who or what tells our hearts to beat approximately sixty to a hundred times per minutes? Where does the power come from to maintain and sustain this rhythm for our entire lives? Who or what empowers our lungs to inhale oxygen and exhale carbon dioxide? What about the other organs in our magnificent bodies? From where comes the intelligence and the power to cause them to function so cooperatively and efficiently in the way they do? What intelligence tells the white corpuscles to rush to our rescue when we cut ourselves? What is the origin of this intelligence? Where is this intelligence located? Is it in our bodies, in our minds or where? We must admit that our bodies are nothing short of being magnificent.

You may be familiar with the wonderful flights that the monarch butterflies take on annually. They fly from Canada and the upper north eastern part of the United States and travel to the Oyamel forests in Mexico. They alight on the trees where they resemble awesomely colorful and beautiful leaves. These butterflies remain there until early October and then they return to their places of origin. What intelligence and power causes these creatures to annually make this trip? How do they know when it is time to make the journey?

What intelligence and power causes birds to know that they can fly or the creatures that they can walk or crawl on the ground or swim in the sea? Where or how did these creatures get this information? How did the salmon learn that, when they are ready to spawn, they must return to the river in which they were born? How do cows know that it can and does produce milk?

These are awesome thoughts and queries of wonderment. But when we consider these ideas, we must admit to being absolutely fascinated with an even larger question—what force created this universe and, maintains and sustains it?

Those of us who are spiritual seekers would respond that the Invisible Presence is the answer to all such questions. We believe that there are many different names for this Presence, but at this stage of my awareness, I am not certain that the name it is given is important. For it seems to be greater than we are in our human state of mind or existence. This presence can be compared to that energy that is used when we plug an appliance into an electrical outlet. We know that energy is invisible; it is a power and we also know that energy causes action to occur.

Not being a scientist or engineer of any sort, I won't even attempt to explain the answers that experts can supply regarding the operational functioning of electricity. But as a person who is aware of and believes in a presence that I call God, I can "see" -- I can accept that there is an invisible presence or power that operates in and through each of us. My experiences and those of so many others has shown me that this invisible presence is within each of us and throughout the entire universe. And regardless of where I am, that presence is always right there with me. No matter where I go, I see the operation of this Presence and Power in all creatures and throughout nature.

Once we become aware of this Invisible Presence, and learn how it operates, we can live different kinds of lives that will prove to be more productive and enjoyable. First, though, we must come to know and learn to trust there is such a power that is available to us.

Many of us have experienced horrific incidents during which there was no external help that we could call upon -- yet intuitively we called on the name of this Invisible Presence, and got a response that saved us from some danger, or we received a healing. I know I can attest to such instances. As students of the universe, we can study and learn about this power.

So I really believe that, if we would take the time to just "check out" this Invisible Presence and see what It can do and how It operates, we might discover that It is real and dependable. We might also learn the laws by which we can work with It. We can thereby create a greater life for ourselves by building a relationship with this power as we get to know more about it. We don't have anything to lose by at least trying it out and seeing what we might learn about life's adventure. We may come to realize that there is some invisible power within us that is also all around us. And we may come to accept that we can use this power for our own and others' highest good. Through our own experiences with this "Invisible Presence", we no longer have to surmise what we have only read or repeat what others have told us, but we can personally confirm that there is something within us that can cause us to demonstrate abundance, health, beauty, creativity, love, and wisdom and more that is far beyond our imagination. But we must be willing to consider the possibility of the existence of an invisible presence and power; begin to trust it and -- ultimately, we will learn that …

"What You See... Is What You Get!"

Chapter 9

ONENESS VS. DUALITY

It is the belief of the mystics of the past centuries that most, if not all, of humanity's difficulties emanate from a belief in two or more powers. We who are engaged in a metaphysical or traditional religion or philosophy, say that we believe in only one God—and one power. Yet, when we look at what is going on in the world, we have to wonder if we really do adhere to a belief in oneness. Or are we still bowing down – at least symbolically – to people and things to which we give power and ask of them favors and blessings to relieve us of our troubles and delivery of some desired good. The reality is that most of us believe in at least one other power (like the devil, otherwise known as satan). Many believe in other powers such as money, jobs, careers, businesses, food, diseases, illnesses, other persons, and things, our bodies—and the list goes on and on.

Without realizing it, we have given our personal power to persons and things outside of ourselves. In the scriptures, we are told that men and women were given dominion over all. But based on our behavior as human beings, it seems obvious that we do not believe only in this one invisible power and presence. In some instances, we were not even taught that this presence was spiritual (in other words, invisible) and that this presence dwells in each of us. Like those of ancient times, we have carved out gods of stone, clay and other materials (like money, gold, other precious metals, etc.) that we, ourselves, created. All over the world, we have made gods of celebrities as many idolize them, claim unreal relationships with and some even go so far as to stalk them. They are idol gods to these persons and they have been given power to control their lives. Although they may not be carved out golden calves as in ancient times, they are still gods unto these people.

One of my favorite biblical stories is that of Daniel in the lions' den. The story is that King Darius of Babylon agreed to create a law stating that no one would be allowed to pray to God and if found to be guilty of this law would be fed to hungry lions. Despite this law, Daniel continued to pray to his God. The wise men administering unto the king knew that Daniel would do this, spied on him and found him praying to his God.

They reported this to the King and so he reluctantly was forced to honor his own decree. Therefore Daniel was placed into the lions' den. On the next morning, everyone expected to see Daniel's carcass spread across the lions' den. However, when the King went to mourn his beloved Daniel, he was astounded and pleased to see that the lions were peacefully lying at the feet of Daniel.

Because of this, King Darius decreed that everyone in his kingdom should give homage to Daniel's God. He declared that, if Daniel's God was powerful enough to save him from those ravenous lions, then that God deserved to be praised by all in his kingdom.

The message of this story is that, if we look to that one God—that one Power—then we all should expect to be cared for, protected, guided, and rescued from the many challenges we face in our daily lives. This is the same message that Jesus spoke of throughout his ministry. When Jesus told Pontius Pilate that he had no power over him other than the power that was given to him from the Invisible Presence (Jesus called him "Father"), he was clear – like Daniel -- that he believed only in the one power and presence. And so when we dedicate ourselves and commit to that one power and presence, we – too – will have the same realization to keep our minds focused on that one power and presence; that is, we should be committed to keeping our minds focused on the One God and not another power which is known as duality.

When we look at nature, we can see the ever-present order and harmony. When we plant an apple seed, we do expect that, in due time, an apple tree will spring forth from the earth and eventually bear apples from the tree. The earth has been revolving around the sun since the beginning of time, and that process has never been altered. Just look at the four seasons and their consistency; these conditions never change. The ebb and flow of the mighty oceans is another constant. We drop something and it always go down. Night and day never change. Regardless of our geographical locations, we all have the same body parts regardless of our race, color or creed.

All the very successful people throughout the world have gained their success through certain principles of success. It doesn't matter what sex they are, what race they are, what creed they may be or how tall or short they may be. There is sameness. The sun, moon, and the stars don't struggle for position. Most birds fly with agility in the air; fish swim in the oceans and seas; snakes crawl along the earth; oranges grow on orange trees; apples on apple trees. Of course, I can go on infinitely about nature's performances, which we mostly take for granted. We expect this order and harmony.

If there were two powers, there would probably be some

inconsistencies in these natural occurrences with which we are so familiar. There might be some dysfunction and a lack of cooperation and systematic order. We could no longer take for granted that on which we currently depend. So with absolute certainty I know that there is only one power—one presence that operates this entire universe. If we say we believe in that one power—that one presence which seems to know what It is doing, and this presence and power demonstrates intelligence and wisdom as well. It shows no preference towards any persons or groups. Given this, I believe that we may safely conclude that we can rely upon this One Universal Source.

It might even be conceivable that, like Daniel, we will survive and continue to live productive, healthy, happy and successful lives. But we must remember that...

"What You See... Is What You Get!"

Chapter 10

"LET GO AND LET GOD

This is the title of a wonderful inspirational song sung by Jack Cassidy, a very talented Christian musician. The message behind the words is very similar to the message of faith. In order for us to "let go and let God," we must trust this entity. So, again, this is a definition of faith. We have already talked about believing or knowing that there is a presence that is all powerful and is everywhere evenly present. Now, if you are not "seeing" this—not understanding or accepting this truth—when different experiences occur in your life, you may believe them to be "coincidences", -- or you may even recognize them as patterns in your life experiences.

Let's assume that you are a believer in this invisible power and you are "seeing" what I am saying, and you are at least in partial agreement with me thus far. By looking at our belief from a logical sense, we are saying that we believe that there is a single power that created the entire universe and all that is in it. We are also believing that this one power or presence minimally has three qualities; which are: 1)omnipresence, (everywhere evenly present), 2) omnipotence (all powerful, and 3) omniscience (all knowing/

wise). Further, we are believing that this one presence and power obviously wants us to express Itself on the visible plane, and by doing so, because It is all that is, It must necessarily create out of Itself. For this reason, we can now assume that we are created out of this Entity and made in Its image and likeness in the same way that we are connected to our biological parents through our DNA. On the invisible level, though, the image and likeness is that of having some similar power such as using our individual minds to create our specific environments and experiences. And this is the critical point, we do have that same power. However, this power is individualized. We can use this powerful tool which is our minds – and use that power to create wonderful worlds for ourselves, and we can positively impact on others as well.

When we stop and realize that we are awesomely created with a power that is within us which no one can take away and no one can adjust in any way, then we can jump for joy with enthusiasm. What a gift! What a valuable tool that each of us has available to us.

Unfortunately, too many of us don't know this truth. We are constantly giving away this gift as we allow others to dictate how we will live our lives. Once we accept this gift as a reality, we can learn to use it in a most positive and joyful way. And when we put our hearts and minds together to change the pollution of hate, envy, disease, lack, and limitation, we can create brand-new worlds for ourselves and help others do the same. We can use the gift of our minds to create loving communities wherever we reside. But this cannot happen unless we can "see" this as our truth. As we accept this as our reality, we will find that ...

"What You See... Is What You Get!"

Chapter 11

A RELATIONSHIP WITH OUR CREATOR

*I*f you are still reading this book, I think I can reasonably assume that we all are on the same page, and we have a basic belief that there is but one Creator of us all, and that includes everything and everyone that is a part of this earthly plane. To help us rationalize or validate this very relevant point of the oneness of us all, I sometimes wonder about certain things such as: throughout the world, every human being has the same bodily appearance; that is, one head, two arms, two legs with the same facial features as well as internal organs. As we look at animals, birds, fish, reptiles, amphibians, and invertebrates, all these creatures of each species have the same general appearances also. We can then surmise that, had there been more than one creative source of everyone and everything, there might be an infinite number of variations of the structures of all species. Of course, the evidence of sameness is infinitely obvious to all who care to take the time to observe—and not take this matter for granted.

Not only do we observe this physical sameness, but there is

also the sameness in our basic needs and desires. I am sure that there is no argument when I state that we all want peace of mind. We all want to have our basic needs met such as decent shelter, clothing, food, and water. Beyond a doubt, we all want to be loved.

Regardless of our culture, nationality, creed, color or race -- we cannot deny this similarity in us all. Would not this imply that there is one Creator of us all? And when we accept and understand the oneness of us all, with one Creator, by recognizing this this could be an opportunity to better our relationships with all people whether or not we are biologically connected.

Intelligence is invisible. Intelligence simply is. When a baby is hungry, even though it doesn't have the words to request its desire for nourishment, it does have the native intelligence to cry out to get its needs met. Also, when a baby's diaper is soiled, it will communicate its discomfort. This is basic native intelligence operating. Earlier we talked about the sameness of all creatures, including human beings. Can we not agree that this one creative source provides all its creations with a level of intelligence to insure their survival. We have discovered that each of these creatures is aware of its specific predators and is able to use it natural defense mechanisms as provided by that creative source. They know how and when to avoid their predators, what foods to eat, and where to find it. I can cite an infinite number of examples of the presence of this thing called intelligence. None can deny the existence of it. Even the tiniest insect displays some level of intelligence. Just observe these little ones when their lives are being threatened. They will exhibit their own level of intelligence in their search for food, their need for safety and their need for a domicile.

So again, we must agree that all creatures have some level of intelligence. And we ask ourselves who or what gives these creatures this gift of intelligence. From where does this intelligence emanate? It is natural for mothers of every species, once their babies are born, to nurture and guide their young ones. We may ponder where does this universal mother response comes from? Who told the mothers to nurture their young? What power caused the mothers' bodies to make adjustments that would not only internally house the growing babies within their bodies, but also prepare the mothers' bodies for nutrition for their young? What power or intelligence causes the mothers to show signs of love, protection, and guidance for their babies. How do the young ones know exactly where to go for their nourishment? What power causes the mothers to physically go out and search for food for their offsprings? How does the mother know when it is time for the young ones to sever themselves from their mothers and become sufficiently independent to begin a life of their own?

I know that these are questions that most of us take for granted. But the answers to these questions definitely imply the oneness of us all and even more importantly the existence of one creator – not two or more.

For myself, I have personally accepted that there is one creator, one presence that is all powerful as well. I am sure that many of you have also reached this conclusion. There is a universal presence that has caused humankind to be of Its highest order of creation. The Scripture tells us that we are made in the "image and likeness" of this awesome creator. We cannot get around the truth that there is an omnipresent, omnipotent, and omniscient presence that is available to us all.

So what is our relationship with this presence? It has created the sun, moon, stars, all of the galaxies, all the creatures that fly in the air, that walk, crawl on earth, and those that swim in the oceans and the seas. Not only does this creative source reveal Its presence, power, and intelligence and It seems to be everywhere we go...available to all.

Even though our parents may no longer be alive, the DNA that they passed along to us at conception can't be altered or severed. That connectiveness is there for eternity. Oneness! That being true on this earthly plane, then would it not be presumed that the same is true on the invisible plane as well? And "spiritual" simply means invisible, nonmaterial, or incorporeal. Whether some want to admit it or not, there is a nonmaterial world. Many scientists today are corroborating the viewpoint that there is an incorporeal creator. There seems to be no other answer other than there is an invisible presence that creates all that we experience on this earthly plane.

None of us has the power to create another being. We are simply open and receptive channels to the experience of the creation of another being.

In accepting the fact that this one power is creative, and as we recognize that we are one with this power, we have the same potential healing our own lives since we are one with that invisible presence. We can never be separate from that creative power just as we can never be separated from the DNA of our physical parents. You don't have to accept my word – just read and study what scientists, mystics and others have discovered. Of course, the Bible declares this is so, but we can always test what may seem like a theory.

You have probably already noticed that when we awaken each morning and decide that it's either going to be a lousy day or that it's going to be a great day. and nothing can deter you from your good mood, your day unfolds as you have predicted—good or bad. However, because most of us don't understand the power that we are, we don't realize that when we used the power of our minds to declare what our day will look like -- we actually began the manifestation of that sort of day. So in the test, let's decide that, for one week, we are going to pay attention to how we use our minds and the correlation or lack thereof between our thoughts and feelings (that is called our consciousness) and the physical manifestation. Amazingly, you will definitely recognize the similarity between your thoughts and feelings and what we experience from day to day.

We have no power over the physical world, but we do have power over our thoughts and feelings. When our thoughts and feelings are concretized on a certain matter, we will find that our experiences seem to match up with them. We can ask ourselves, "What causes that correlation? Again, some of us who are not willing to open up to further consideration other than it may just be a coincidence will definitely miss the picture. However, those of us who take the opportunity to inquire on a deeper level will discover that there seems to be an invisible presence that can and does impose Itself upon our lives in accordance with the way we see and think about our daily lives. Succinctly stated, we experience the daily activities of our individual lives according to ...

"What You See... Is What You Get!"

Chapter 12

POWER OF PRAYER

*D*o we really believe in the power of prayer? We are told that prayer is talking to or with God. However, in order for us to pray to a power that we believe will respond to our requests, we have to believe or feel that that presence can and will answer our prayers. Do we believe that this presence is even interested in helping us in our times of need? As I read the scriptures, I am reminded that whenever Jesus healed a person of some ailment, he would always ask some form of the question, "Do you believe that I can do this?" And when the person responded in a positive manner, the healing took place regardless of what the condition, situation, or circumstance may have existed. In the same manner, when we purchase a household product, there is always an owner's manual that provides instructions on how to install and care for the product. And personally, I believe that the Bible is our owners' manual helping us to recognize that there are specific laws (spiritual) and if followed will cause us to live more successful lives.

Previously, we talked about looking out at nature and asking questions like how do the seeds that we plant in the soil know that it is an orange tree that we expect to manifest? How are all the parts of an orange tree ultimately produced? What causes the roots, the trunk, the branches, the leaves, and the fruit to show up in due season? Did the person who planted the seeds have to pray for this seeming miracle to occur? If not, what power or presence caused this orange tree to manifest in its perfection? Why didn't the planter of the seeds have to pray for the seeds to germinate? I continue to throw out these kinds of questions for our broader consideration so that we do not continue to take this life adventure for granted. It really doesn't matter what we may call this entity -- be it God, supreme power, invisible presence, divine mind, or whatever -- each of us has the privilege of making this choice with which we are most comfortable. Yet I recognize that each of us has to "see" for ourselves that this invisible something is real to you. Otherwise, why would we, as rational and intelligent human beings, try to develop a relationship with something we have only heard about? It just doesn't make sense, does it? So even the most doubting mind must admit that there may be a correlation between what we perceive and what we experience in our lives.

"What You See... Is What You Get!"

Chapter 13

WHO IS / WHAT IS "I AM"?

*W*e all refer to ourselves as "I." There's no way we can refer to another person and use the statement, "I am." We can share with others and indicate thoughts like these: I am beautiful.; I am happy; I am tall; I am unhappy; I am successful;. I am lonely. So, when we speak to others about ourselves and say, "I am," we are not referring to our legs, arms, feet, or any other parts of our bodies -- but rather we are referencing that invisible component of ourselves that is hard to explain but it is that essential aspect of ourselves with which we all are familiar. In those instances when we say, "I am" that is just an indication of our individuality which is unique and unrepeatable. We know, for sure, that even with twins (although they may appear physically identical) we should be aware that there are some individual differences which makes each twin unique in their own way! That difference, I believe, is the I am within themselves. So when we say, "I am," we are announcing the recognition, understanding, and acceptance of that something that is within us. That something is invisible, of course. How we identify this aspect of ourselves really determines what our life experiences will look like. If people believe and have much confidence in themselves, there is nothing that can deter them from attaining whatever goals they set out for themselves. Their thoughts about that inner "I am" will determine their life styles. A person who says "I am beautiful" will carry himself or herself in a manner that reflects that belief. What a powerful announcement of self. However, that person who has a timid and passive sense of self (their I am), they will have a completely different life experiences.

Whatever your belief system is about yourself (that I am), you will either be in charge of your life or you will give others the power to impact on your life. The fascinating thing about our "I am" is that no one gave it to us; no one can make adjustments to it and no one can take it away from us. Whatever adjustments we want to make, it is entirely up to each of us. You and you alone can determine whether you are beautiful, intelligent, creative or whatever you decide it is that you want to be. It's all about you!

In the scriptures, we are told that God directed Moses to lead the Hebrew children out of Egypt. But Moses asked God "What if I am asked who sent me? What should I tell them? And God's response to this query was: "Tell them that "I Am That I Am" hath sent you. That is what we know as God: I Am That I Am. That is a complete statement! If you are ever in the midst of some devastating situation, and you have the wherewithal to yell out with all of your heart and soul, "I am in the presence of God" or "I am safe!" or "I am protected!" I can practically guarantee you that you will most likely walk away – completely safe from any harm or danger to yourself! This has been my personal experience in several occasions. You might not be completely unscathed, but you will survive the incident in a far better manner than had you not declared your "I am" awareness. The affirmation or declaration "I am in in the presence of God" is a declaration that will empower and protect you from the elements of any unfavorable incidents. Whatever level of awareness that you may have of that I am within you will determine how successfully you walk and carry yourself on this earthly plane. I would not make this statement unless I knew it to be the absolute truth.

I have personally encountered several life-threatening experiences in which I adamantly declared who I believed that I am. And in making that declaration, I obviously had expectations that ultimately enabled me to survive each instance in a most satisfactory manner. In each of these instances, I focused on what I believe is the truth of my being—what I think about myself. "I am a child of God. I am in the presence of God. I am guided and protected. I am loved." And others. These statements reflect what I think I am or my state of being. In each case, what I saw or believed about myself -- made all the difference regarding the outcome of all these life-threatening experiences. So over the years, I have come to realize that, yes, for sure ...

"What You See... Is What You Get!"

Chapter 14

WORRY 101

$\mathcal{W}$e don't realize that our thoughts, which are another form of energy, are definitely creative. Imagine pouring water into a tall, thin glass or a short, wide glass, or a bottle shaped like a fish! The water, of course, takes on the shape of the vessel that contains it. This is somewhat like what happens when we take on thoughts of worry, anxiety and fear. In fact though, this is what occurs with every thought we have particularly those that we consistently harbor in our minds.

Every day of our lives, scientists tell us that we have about 70,000 thoughts concerning the present moment, the past, and of course, the future. As a former educator, I have had many conversations with young people who were just about to graduate from high school and really wanted to attend college. However, in some of these instances, they advised me that they had decided not to attend college because they didn't want to go into a lot of debt in order to get their degrees. So, in these instances, they had already begun to worry about the high cost of education and therefore could not envision a possible solution to their seeming problem of high indebtedness. Because of their belief that there would not be a way for them to get a grant, a gift from someone or some other kind of financial assistance, they were unable to even consider the possibility of a viable solution to this problem. They had already begun to worry about not being able to pay off their college loans, and so they decided to not even try to make the effort. They were blocked even before they got started because of their limited vision and state of worry. They were prevented from attending college only because they could not "see" the possibility of something wonderful happening to support them in achieving the desire of their hearts.

If they were aware of unlimited possibilities, they would have been open to other alternatives. For example, when I decided that I wanted to complete my graduate degree, it never occurred to me that even though my undergraduate degree had not yet been paid off and, in fact, due to some totally unexpected financial difficulties, the loan was actually in default. My only concern was that I needed some financial support (a student loan) to accomplish this goal. I gave no consideration to the status of the earlier loan, I applied for a second student loan. Both friends and relatives literally laughed at my seeming naivete – -- the audacity of believing that I would be approved for a second student loan was beyond their comprehension. My only thought was that I needed or wanted a means to complete my masters' degree. I did not allow those surrounding me to taint my vision, so I applied and two years later, I walked away from Hunter College in NYC with a M.A. degree in Education. Had I listened to the naysayers or those who had limited vision or had I worried about the problem as in the example stated above, my story may very well have been quite different from what actually occurred. But I did not worry. I had a different vision.

Shortly after graduation, I attained a teaching position in what was then called an "At Risk" district. Due to this designation, I was told by the Fanny Mae student loan division that I would not have to re-pay either of my outstanding loans. Additionally all the teachers in this district were given a 15% to 18% increase in salary! Over the years, I have shared this and other similar experiences where I did not worry about some pending event, but kept my mind focused on what I wanted to achieve rather than worry about what might happen. I have come to realize that worry only blocks my ability to think creatively and expansively. In many of my lectures, this is a humorous way of conveying this idea – and – it is this: "If worry could ever assist me in any way, I would be teaching a course at Columbia University in NYC called "Worry 101".

In the example that I described earlier, these people did not understand that the act of worrying about anything only serves us in limiting our desired good. Without an awareness of or a consciousness of "I have got to give it a try and see what happens," you will miss so much of what that life force can do for you. So now I tell all who will listen to me that, if worrying about something proved to be helpful at all, I would be teaching Worry 101 at Columbia University in New York City.

Now it is so clear to me that the habit of worrying is so limiting and so deprecating, and it takes joy away from us; we become de-energized and lifeless. I am now certain that worry brings about only sorrow and joylessness. It causes us to falsely believe that we are alone, worthless, and powerless. Worrying about anything at all only brings about lack and limits our joy and greater expression of our good. So for sure, I know that …

"What You See... Is What You Get!"

Chapter 15

THE ONENESS OF US ALL

*M*ost humans simply live their lives as if there is nothing more than what their five senses tell them what is going on. And ignorantly, we believe that the five senses always tell us the truth. But that is certainly not the case. At one time in mankind's history, it was believed that the sun revolved around the earth. Then there was a false belief that the moon was a flat disk and that the stars were just little bits of light. None of these former beliefs is true. So our five senses have lied to us about these matters and so many more for so, so long.

I once heard a woman say that we have to be sick! And that is a belief of too many of the world's population. So a great deal of research has been conducted in some of our major and highly respected universities and institutions of higher education throughout the world, and what they discovered was that our state of mind determines our health and also our life experiences.

However, I believe that we all have a sixth sense (some call it intuition) that tells us that there is something else— something other than what our physical selves reveal to us. I say this because, in spite of the false belief that we are not related to any others and we are on this earthly journey struggling, suffering, loving, playing, all by ourselves, I have come to realize that there is that "something" within each of us that denies this false idea of separation from all others. The truth that there is something in this universe of which all of us are a part.

When we take the time to observe our biological siblings and other family members, we can certainly attest to physical similarities. And at other times, when there is no biological connectedness, we can still see our reflections in others as well. Did you ever ask yourself why is this? Further, if you would take the time to observe these similarities—likes and dislikes, desires and goals—between you and others who are not biologically affiliated with you, you may query why or what is the basis of these similarities. Even the form and the operation of our human bodies are the same. Reproduction of all is the same. If we look at nature, we will see the sameness. Within the animal world, when one dog encounters another dog they seem to instinctively know their sameness and they (in most cases) begin to sniff each other. Did you ever ponder why doesn't a dog attempt to react in the same manner to a nearby pigeon or a cat? What intelligence or power causes each dog to recognize its counterpart. Even in human beings, did you ever notice that babies also recognize each other? This, I believe, is further evidence of some invisible power or source that is operating in the universe. We see these occurrences but we are so used to them, that we mostly don't question them.

However, if we would stop to query further, we would probably see the similarity among us all. In 1944, an experiment was conducted with 40 newborn babies all of whom were physically healthy. All of their physiological needs were met; that is, they were fed, properly clothed, and bathed. During this experiment, however, caretakers made no show of affection toward the babies, no eye contact, no touching of any kind. This experiment lasted for four months, and during that time, some of the babies died. Those who survived the experiment, seemed to be lifeless. They made no effort to verbalize; they became "vegetables" just lying there. There were no physical reasons why this occurred. At the same time, in another part of this facility, 20 babies were given their physical needs, but they were also provided with their emotional, psychological and spiritual needs as well. All of these babies abundantly thrived.

From this and other examples, what conclusion can we draw about the oneness of us all? Humans need love; we need to be touched and emotionally nurtured. Even those human beings who have committed the most heinous crimes have these affective needs. Why is this true? I believe that it is true because there is "something" within each of us that is the source of our oneness. This source is apparent in the animal world and in the world of humans – claiming our need to prove our oneness with each other.

When we come to understand and accept this oneness of us all, we will "see" that this recognition of the truth will bring about closer and more harmonious relationships among us all. I believe that our recognition of the oneness of us all will help bring about the "peace of the world" that we all desire. So ...

"What You See... Is What You Get!"

Chapter 16

LIFE'S UNIVERSITY

*O*n the physical plane, most of us begin our formal education around the age of four, and this may continue on to the graduate level and beyond. I know for myself that, after completing my master's degree ; obtaining certifications from two metaphysical institutions, and the constant need to attend workshops and seminars in order to stay abreast of the ever-changing teaching practices, I ultimately got to a point where I was feeling, *No more classes … No more school for me!*

However, when it comes to spiritual development, that is not an option. Each day we are alive, whether we choose to or not there is that daily call to participate in the classes of life. These classes consist of our daily interactions with each other, performing in our jobs and careers, and functioning in our different roles as parents, friends, lovers, co-workers, and strangers. And most importantly, we learn to keep watch over our thoughts, feelings, speech, and actions, for these are the factors that determine what our life experiences will look like. We recognize that, if we have not been paying attention in our classes of life studies, our lives will reflect that inattention. And that will show up as a life that is filled with lots of frustration, anger, lack of peace, and much dissatisfaction and struggle in our lives—lives that are lived without a joyful purpose on earth.

So ultimately we may come to realize that there is no graduation from this life university when it comes to our spiritual development. We simply go from class to class, awakening to or becoming more deeply aware of this awesome place in which we reside. Other than interacting with each other are the additional teachers which are those ever-occurring events, conditions, and circumstances in our lives. Even those with whom we have no immediate and physical interaction -- which is that collective universal beliefs --that impact on our own thoughts and feelings and become the cause of our own personal life experiences.

For example, there is a universal collective belief that if we get caught in a heavy rain without proper attire, we will definitely suffer and "catch" a cold. Another example would be our universal belief that come the flu season, we should expect to either catch the flu or prepare to ward off the infection. In order for us to be more successful in every aspect of our lives, we should pay closer attention to what's happening in our life classes; that is, our lives. I know many people – and perhaps you do as well – who continue to have the same kinds of undesirable experiences. However because we are not paying attention or we are ignorant of the fact that we are always students in this university of life. So there is never a graduation. We continue to experience these undesirable situations, conditions and circumstances until we have learned the necessary lesson.

I have a friend who was having similar unfavorable experiences on her different jobs. At first, she wasn't paying attention, but then she recognized an apparent pattern and saw that she was the

Portia A. Jones

person who was common in each situation with which she was confronted. She began to understand that in order to positively alter her life, she had to change her thinking, emotions and behavior. In one particular instance, the confrontation involved an East Indian female co-worker. On another occasion, she was confronted by a Caucasian male and in another instance, an African-American female was involved. Over the years, these incidents continued until she began to notice a pattern; that is, some similarities in all of these occasions. She stopped complaining about these incidents and blaming the other persons. She recognize that in each instance, the commonality in every situation, was, of course, herself. She began to understand that life is, indeed, a university where we always have an opportunity to learn new life lessons. Ultimately she came to see that each of those co-workers was a teacher for her and that she would most likely continue to have these kinds of experiences until she learned the lesson she needed to learn. So she worked with herself to learn the necessary lesson; that is, she looked at her state of mind—her thoughts and feelings. The process took time because she discovered that these confrontations were based on old thoughts and feelings that had nothing to do with her teachers. They were just there to assist her in her spiritual growth and to become a more wonderful and loving person. She got it. Her life changed considerably in this area, but the major lesson that she said she received is that living life is a constant class attendance and it is absolutely essential to "pay attention".

The opportunities for our spiritual growth—our greater understanding of our relationship with the Creator of all—is constant. Coming to the realization that our relationship with each other and our spiritual Father/Mother/God remains with us as well. I honestly believe that that invisible presence, because of its constant forgiving and loving nature, allows us the freedom to choose whether we learn from these experiences or not. This presence, I believe, *never* forces us to "get it". We have the power within ourselves to change our minds at any given time.

Therefore, we always have options. For most of us, and unlike the way it is in our physical schools, we cannot drop out. There's something about that life force within us that keeps nudging us to "hang on" to the life that we have been given. In our earthly classes, we do have the freedom to limit our classroom attendance and how much we bring to the classroom in our participation and attention. Interestingly enough, we have the same options available to us. And in both cases, we get out of it – what we invest in. Whether we agree or not, whether we understand or not, our every encounter with others is a divine opportunity to learn something wonderful about ourselves. When we have negative encounters with others, we tend to point our fingers and accuse them; that is, it is much easier for us to blame others rather than take the time (opportunity) to look at ourselves and ponder what part did we play in causing this negative experience. Rarely do we blame ourselves. And I have learned not to place blame even on ourselves, but simply take the time to pay attention; observe and take responsibility for the part we may have played in each scenario. We recognize, of course, that we cannot change other people; we can only change ourselves. The experience amounts to being our teachers. And, at the same time, if that other person understands how life works for us all, they – too – may come to understand that each encounter – all of our life experiences are wonderful lessons that show up to help us become greater than we seem to be. Unknowingly, we all agree to play various roles in each others 'lives to help us to become wiser and possibly more compassionate in our interaction with each other through these life learning experiences. So if we understood this, we would no longer get angry with another person, we would sincerely say "thank you" for helping me become a greater being who I am destined to be.

Scriptures says that we are created in the image and likeness of God, and so we have a God-given power to create what we want to manifest in our lives. Understanding, of course, as Jesus taught that, on our own, we can do nothing, but it is the power within us that causes us to do all things. As I stated before, life is a constant place of learning, and we have the potential within ourselves to create the kinds of life experiences that will support and ultimately bring about our hearts' desires. And this includes not only our careers, our residences, all of our relationships, and certainly our health and our wealth as well; that is, every aspect of our lives.

Even with all of my spiritual classes, workshops, and readings, I have not always been a totally conscious and dedicated student of life. I forget sometimes, but what I have learned is that none of the spiritual laws change for me. Spiritual laws – like earthly laws – are quite impersonal and really operate for all of our highest good. Only when I make a conscious decision to pay attention to my lessons and give thanks to all of my teachers and decide to continue to commit myself to learning the lessons that the life force intends for me to learn am I the satisfied person who is ever striving to become the absolute best that I can be. Now I forget less and remember more quite definitely that life can be and is wonderful, and it is truly up to me for that to happen. This is my belief, and I see the evidence of this belief every day from the so-called small to the major events and interactions in my life. I have come to recognize that …

"What You See... Is What You Get!"

Chapter 17

THOUGHTS ARE THINGS

*I*n Proverbs 23:7 we are told that "For as he thinketh in his heart, so is he."

"Thoughts Are Things" is the title of a book by Dr. Ernest Holmes in which he states a theory that our thoughts are a kind of energy and as long as they are maintained and are coupled with similar feelings, these thoughts will ultimately be concretized as actual experiences in our lives. Holmes is the founder of the metaphysical teaching called Religious Science also known as Science of Mind (not to be confused with Ron Hubbard's philosophy termed, "Scientology"). Most of us recognize that there are conscious thoughts that come up throughout the day. Neuroscientists discovered that we actually think about 10,000 to 70,000 on a daily basis. We recognize that some of those thoughts get pushed down into another part of our minds called the subjective or subconscious mind. These are the thoughts that can and do cause our lives to look a certain way -- either negatively or positively. We have come to realize that our thoughts can cause us to be happy or sad, healthy or sick, wealthy or poor. These thoughts can cause us to be a doctor or a homeless person or anything in between.

The author, Napoleon Hill was inspired and commissioned in 1937 by business magnate Andrew Carnegie to interview men who turned out to be extremely wealthy while many others were experiencing poverty. After completing this assignment, Hill garnered all his information and compiled his data into a book entitled, *"Think and Grow Rich"*. This book is still being used in colleges and universities throughout the country and has recently re-surfaced in popularity among those who are looking at how the mind impacts on one's business and career success. Based on Hill's interviews, he discovered that there was a commonality among these highly successful men. And that commonality was the manner in which they approached situations and conditions in their lives. Regardless of what challenges they were confronted with, they always believed in their ability to solve every problem. They never allowed themselves to give up -- they never saw impossibilities. All of these men obtained outrageous wealth -- even in times when others were experiencing dire poverty; specifically during the economic challenges of the early 1920's -- like the depression. As we read his book, we see that each man's thoughts or his perspective on life made all the difference in how his life unfolded and impacted on their own lives, the lives of those not only in this country, but the world at large. Each of these men helped to change the world, making it easier for us to accomplish simple tasks in our daily affairs. Their thoughts propelled them to speak and act in a certain manner. All of the men who were interviewed thought highly of themselves, the world and its possibilities. They all felt that they had the power to effect change despite what was going on in their present environments. Some of these men started out with "silver spoons" in their mouths, while others had to "pull themselves up by their bootstraps" to effect the changes in the world. So it was not about the conditions of their births or their environments; rather, it was about what these "movers and shakers" thought about themselves and their abilities to make a difference in the world.

These men's prosperous thoughts helped them to invent businesses and products that impacted on the world's economic systems. All of these world changes occurred as a result of the power of the thoughts of these successful men. Thoughts are a dynamic form of energy. So certainly, we can conclude that, indeed, thoughts are things!

Near the turn of the 19th century, there were many people who were praying and worrying about the lack of horses, which was then the primary source of transportation. These worriers did not know that there were men who had gotten the idea of the possibility of creating a motorized vehicle. Men like Karl Benz, Nicholas-Joseph Cugnot and Henry Ford – all of these men and others as well -- were in the midst of changing history relative to transportation. So at one time, these were just thoughts... of course, these thought later became things (as Dr. Ernest Holmes wrote).

I truly believe that there is a power called thought. Even though thought is an invisible entity, it is, nevertheless, a powerful energy. And each of us has this awesome power that is available to us at all times. We can use this power to not only change our personal lives but also to help others to change the lives as well.

So whether we believe it or not, thoughts are a powerful energy that can definitely and does change our lives. Therefore we must at least come to consider this possibility of truth that...

"What You See... Is What You Get!"

Chapter 18

THE MOST POWERFUL TOOL WE HAVE (THE MIND VIEWED ANOTHER WAY)

For certain, during our earthly journey, we will have many adventures, for life is, indeed, an adventure. Some aspects of this adventure will be pleasant and others not so pleasant. However, it is up to each of us to determine how we will react or respond to all of our life experiences. The tool that is absolutely unrelentingly powerful is – our minds. This applies to every aspect of our lives, and it doesn't matter whether we encounter disease, poverty, or inharmonious relationships. Our state of mind determines what is going to happen to us. Years ago, I witnessed a United States senator being interviewed by a T.V. reporter who had not been re-elected for another term in office. His home had recently burned down, and he was preparing to declare bankruptcy. The reporter asked the senator how he felt about all the misfortunes that he and his family had recently experienced. The senator replied that as long as he had a mind that was fully functional, he would be able to create an abundant life for himself and his family again.

I was absolutely floored and impressed by this senator's state of mind. He understood something that too many people don't recognize; that is, that our state of minds (state of consciousness) makes all the difference in our lives. This senator clearly understood that he was in charge of his life. He did not judge by the appearances, but he wisely chose to use the power within himself to re-build his life. It is definitely up to each of us to use our powerful minds to overcome negativity and not allow the conditions, situations and circumstances to dictate to us what our lives are going to look like.

We all have read stories of athletes and others (both men and women) who overcame physical and mental challenges that did interrupt and could have prevented their not being able to attain their original goals and dreams. Nonetheless with seeming miraculous tenacity and will power they were able to respond rather than react to their life situations. I now call these --- "opportunities." For, indeed, that's what they are.

These challenges show up in our lives as teachers and opportunities giving us a chance to learn about and use the power that is within us. Had not they occurred in our lives, we may not have come to realize the greatness that is within us. As mentioned before, the thoughts in our invisible minds are the most powerful tools that we all have available to us, at all times throughout the day and wherever we are. So if we ask ourselves how we see each aspect of this adventure (called life) that is constantly confronting us, we can start by admitting to the facts; then we can proceed by reminding ourselves that we have an invaluable tool -- although invisible --available to us. No one gave it to us and no one can make adjustments to it or take it away from us.

Like Napoleon Hill, if we would take the time to observe the lives of those men and women whom we mostly admire due to the successes they have obtained in their chosen fields of interest, we will be able to see that it wasn't about some capricious thing called "luck" but rather it was a matter of how these individuals took their lives by the horns (took action) and caused their desired dreams and goals to manifest in their lives. Listen to the words of these heroes and heroines, and you will see that their positive results were due to the culmination of thoughts, their feelings and specific actions -- all of which were generated by their states of mind. It was never a matter of their being physically stronger or wiser than others. Rather, It was simply a matter of how they used the power of their minds in given situations to attain the good which they desired.

A friend forwarded this quote to me by an unknown author, a portion of which I want to share with you: "In life, you will realize there is a role for everyone you meet. Some will test you, some will use you, some will love you, but all will teach you."

She sent this to me after an event that had occurred between another person and me. In that encounter, I was being accused of an unfavorable behavior. As this person confronted me with her perception of this incident, my state of mind was simply one of being a listener. I had no need to defend or explain myself. I later realized that there was something on a deeper level for me to learn from this experience. After much thought, getting still and prayer, I came to understand that the person who had blamed me of improper behavior was saying to me that my behavior towards her caused her not to feel loved. Although that was certainly not my intention, I had offended her. So I forgave myself and began to feel more empathy toward this person rather than being angry or annoyed by her accusations. I had a better understanding that her state of mind not my words and action – were possibly reminders of some unhappy occasions that had occurred in her life and;

therefore caused her to feel unloved. Unfortunately I provoked some negative emotions that had not been resolved in her mind and heart. I actually felt gratitude towards this person because she had become, my teacher. For there was a time in my own life when I have pointed my finger at others for something I thought they had done to me. Although we sometimes do but probably on a subconscious level, offend others. Sometimes when others blame us, we should not just summarily dismiss them, but take the opportunity to become more mindful of our own thoughts and feelings. Whether we know it or not, there is a spiritual law called the Law of Attraction; that is, we attract what our consciousness is like – very much like a magnet. So each event in our lives, reveal to us that which we have been focusing on either consciously or subconsciously.

I am and you are responsible for what we want to experience in life. And the beauty of this is that we have the power within us to do just that. Ignorantly (meaning not knowing) though, and often times without this knowledge we blame others for our misfortunes and fail to look at ourselves to where the answer really lies. That's how we mis-use and abuse others. In essence we are doing this to ourselves. We are depriving ourselves of greater awareness of the power that is within ourselves...missing out on our own greatness.

However, as we begin to read, study, and practice according to our expanding mind sets, we become more aware of that power within us which we can use always for our and others' highest good. We will begin to learn that the most valuable tool that we have available to us is our minds...our thoughts. When we come to see – to understand -- this, we learn to make conscious and wiser decisions that will positively impact on our and others' lives. We learn to take the time out of our busy schedules to get still and allow our minds to settle down in the quietness. This, of course, we call meditation.

So, when we come to understand or "see" that there is an awesome power that is within each of us, we can begin to bring about for ourselves and others more joy-filled, healthy and abundant lives.

"What You See... Is What You Get!"

Chapter 19

IT WAS JUST MY IMAGINATION

There is a wonderful song that was written by Norman Whitfield and Barrett Strong and performed by the famous singing group, the Temptations. The title of the song is "It Was Just My Imagination." We use our imaginations and don't really understand the power of this tool. Our imaginations are just another awesome way of using our powerful minds to create more and greater good in our lives. Interestingly enough, we seem not to have any problem with using our imaginations in creating negative events in our lives; yet, I believe that we are ignorant of the fact that we are using this powerful tool that is ever available for our use – be it for the negative or positive. Our minds can take us from high to medium to low. We can actually use our imaginations to create whatever experiences we may or may not want. Children are great at using their imaginations. Unfortunately, though, we unwisely teach our children not to use this powerful tool.

If you are interested or at least care to test out this theory, you can try it out for yourself. First decide what good you want to show up in your life. A very important point, though, is that you must make sure that the good you desire is not taking away from or harming another person in any way. The universe can sufficiently provide for everyone! You must also make a conscious decision to at least temporarily suspend any doubts that you may have during this experiment; that is, suspend all questions about the use of your imagination. Doubt, fear, worry, and anxiety are definite "blockers" when we are using our imaginations. If you are familiar with this process, then you already know and can testify to the validity of what I am saying. However, if you are new to this way of thinking, I would suggest that you come up with something that is relatively small in nature that you may have previously believed was beyond your ability to achieve (like passing a seemingly difficult exam, acquiring a car, a house or a better position at your work-place).

You see, our minds are a kind of energy which I have already talked about. As I have previously stated, children naturally use this mechanism all the time until the adults in their lives convince them that "… they should be more realistic."

So the process is that you must become absolutely certain that that which you are imaging can become a physical reality and is within the realm of natural law. On this you must be very clear. Train yourself to be in an expectant state of mind and act as if someone has promised you some desired good. It's like placing an order at an invisible store, and even though you don't know the exact delivery date, you are sure that the expected good will be delivered any day now. Of course, you must not become anxious about the delivery date. Just be certain that delivery of your good is certain. Be sure not to expect your good to come by way of any particular person or in any particular manner. Take the time -- at least two times every day -- to think about how you would feel if that desired good were presented to you at this very moment. You must feel and not just mentally notice it but practice using your imagination to acquire this good. Children do this naturally. Even go far as to act as if the good is already yours.

When I was relatively new to this metaphysical teaching, I did try the process. I wanted a new car. So I went to a car dealership; told the salesperson what kind of car I desired and then we took a test drive. After the salesperson and I returned from the test drive, he went into another office to check my credit score and came back with a saddened face. He indicated to me that due to my credit score, I would not qualify to receive a loan to purchase the car of my choice which was a Berlinetta (Chevy Camaro). He stated, however, that he could sell me a previously owned Volkswagen. I declined his kindly offer and declared to him, "Watch me" as I left his office. For the next two months, I used my imagination and pictured myself driving around town in my new Berlinetta. I wasn't going to allow the physical reality to block my good. So like a child, I visualized my desired good and I even included the specific details that I wanted in my new car.

Around the beginning of a three-month period, I was the proud owner of a new Berlinetta with the added features that I had pictured in my mind!

Those who are familiar with the metaphysical philosophy and teaching know this process as visualization; anyone who is imaginative enough and is open and receptive to the utilization of this tool will discover that it can be fun and is useful (if you can believe) in bringing about all the good that you can imagine.

Some people use what is called a "vision board" or a regular three-ring notebook using pictures that are cut out from a magazine representing their desired good. I think most don't understand why or how this process works but it absolutely does work and maybe the most difficult aspect of this process is the letting go of the doubt and believing in the process. Those who are successful in this process, even call it a miracle. To the skeptics or those of a no non-sense personality, it's just a senseless effort or activity for the weak in mind or is viewed as just New Age foolishness or "airy fairy".

You don't have to accept the metaphysical philosophy or teaching, but I can assure you that this process works, and many can testify to its validity. This process just works because it has to do with how our minds work. For those who have told me that they have tried it and it didn't work for them, I share with them that they probably didn't get their minds and emotions engaged to the point of where they truly believed that this was possible. It has to do with believing. If we do our part, the universe always does its part.

We all use the power called electricity. Most of us who use this wonderful power can't explain the specifics of how or why it works, but we know it works and so we all have availability to this awesome power called electricity. Most of us don't understand nor can we explain (certainly not I) the mechanics of the engine of an automobile, but we have no problem driving our cars or turning on the electrical appliances in our homes. Most of us can't explain the laws of aerodynamics, yet that doesn't prevent us from booking a flight to fly all across the country or the world. My reason for mentioning this is obvious, or course. In this almost unbelievable age of technology, we cannot explain how the many electronic devices function – yet most of us are now taking for granted all these new and marvelous discoveries which have made our lives easier and more convenient. So again, my point is that just because we can't explain or it's new to us, we should not be so closed minded of the possibility of a new discovery of which we are not familiar or cannot explain how it functions. The difference, here of course, may be this process called visualization or the use of our minds to bring about our needs and desires without our having to struggle for it. We do, of course, use our minds every day but not in this deliberate and conscious way. If there is a possibility of our being introduced to a new idea called "imagination", or "visualization" why not try it with an open mind. So, regarding the power of our imagination, it should not matter whether we can or cannot explain how this process works. As Nike states, "Just do it!"

Modern day humanity has advanced so tremendously during these last few centuries in inventing products to make our lives easier. Yet when it comes to looking at the human mind -- I don't believe that we have made advances to the same degree. Most of us have not come to a place of understanding and accepting that our minds are an awesome reservoir of energy. Many scientists have done so -- but certainly not the general populace throughout the world. We really do have available to us the use of a universal gift—a personal energy or power that those inventors uncovered and they recognize that this energy is accessible for all of us and individually. History tells us most of the inventors like Henry Ford, Thomas Edison, Alexander Graham Bell, Marconi, Galileo, Columbus and so many others were met with criticism, derision, and disbelief when they initially presented their ideas to the general population, yet their discoveries ultimately changed the whole world. Those inventors were visionaries and believed beyond what they already knew as facts. So, as visionaries, they used their imaginations, and they all attained exactly what they saw in their imaginations or their minds' eyes, so they must have learned that…

"What You See... Is What You Get!"

Chapter 20

THE POWER OF OUR WORDS

As kids, we were taught by our parents and teachers that the words we use do, indeed, have the power to hurt others. When I was a youngster, we could hear children chanting, "Sticks and stones may hurt my bones, but names will never hurt." Others' words can have a negative or positive impact on us. But what is the truth about the power of the words that we speak and hear? Words are the audible expression of our thoughts. So you see we are still talking about that same power as discussed earlier—our thoughts.

Actually, it's not the words of themselves that have the power, but rather what images we conjure up in our minds when we hear hurtful or healing words.

These words may be positive or negative and the images that are formed in one's mind are powerful stimuli that mostly relate to some past experiences that were very impactful. When people talk to us, we actually create images connected to those words. Some say that we see with our minds.

We can't get away from my earlier premise that we are, indeed, spiritual beings. And, as such, we use our power— our energy—and our words to create or to destroy. This is all within our purview. Yet like any other power or energy, we can't see it. Nevertheless, this power is always functioning. Since this power (like all others) is invisible, we should learn more about it and its operation. If we accept that knowledge is power, then as we learn more about this particular power, we may become more proficient in utilizing it for our higher good. Let's suppose that someone hears: "The stove was burning hot!" Even as you read these words, you probably visualized a burning stove. So the imagery that the hearer creates in his mind is a stovetop and probably the color red, which is an indication of intense heat. Or someone might hear: "I was dead tired." The imagery that we conjure up might be a person collapsing onto a sofa or bed, completely exhausted. Or possibly someone removing his or her shoes, plopping listlessly onto a nearby chair or sofa, and relaxing his or her head on the back of that chair or sofa. Two short sentences — five or less words can cause a person to conjure up in his or her mind stories that may cause pain and suffering or these same words may be the stimulus for joy and laughter. So it is not actually the words themselves that have the power to impact on others, but the words can and do assist us to trigger memories that can help to bog us down or lift us up. Therefore in that sense, words can help or harm others.

Given these examples, you probably were able to discern exactly what I mean when I say that our words have power. Why? Because we give power to the words by using our ability to create. The power is within us and not in the words themselves.

The millennial generation uses words that have completely different meaning than the meanings understood by the boomer or the silent generations. Examples like: lit, phat, dope or salty. So obviously, the power is not in the words; rather the power is within ourselves. The belief that words have power over us and can harm us or cause us to be negatively or positively impacted is, I believe, a false concept. But, of course, I believe that, on this particular point, many will disagree with me. However, if those who disagree with me care to take the time to investigate what I believe and discover for themselves whether my words are true or not, they may very well come to see that what I am saying is indeed true. For those, I will share another example of the so-called power of words. When I was a child, if someone called an African-American person "black", that was time to fight. And I personally heard the exchange of many angry words and saw several physical fights and certainly a lot of anger because someone was called, "black". And this word was used for the very purpose of evoking anger. Today, however, it is quite acceptable for those of the African-American community to be called, "black". So the power has not changed and the word has not changed; rather, our belief system about that word *and so many others* has changed. At this time in history, due to the development of technology, we have a reservoir of vocabulary that was not even apparent a few years ago. Many who consider themselves feminists created the word *herstory* to represent history from a feminist point of view or emphasizing women's contributions to the development of our and other countries.

Here's another example: When I entered junior high school, my teacher selected several students, including me, that we would be her top-achieving algebra students. Initially I thought that she was joking. She couldn't possibly believe that I would be a top-notch algebra student. Math certainly wasn't my strength; I had always had to work very hard to maintain good grades in math. At the end of the school year, however, I had proven her prediction right. We all know just how important it is to use positive words to encourage and support our children. I believe that I heard her words and made a decision to either impress her or not to embarrass myself. To some, this example may seem as if the words, themselves were – indeed -- powerful. No doubt this teacher's words were a stimuli; however, it could have gone either way. My personality, my particular state of mind or how this young child interpreted those words. Hence, I believe that it is not the particular words themselves, but how one's words are taken into our own imagery.

The reason I put this out for further consideration is that I honestly believe that we take far too much for granted, and we fail to dig deeper into what is really going on within ourselves and this prevents us from being greater than what we think are and can be. We limit ourselves from being our true and greater selves.

The power was not necessarily in the words that the teacher spoke, I believe that all along, the power was within that little girl who had always had difficulty in mastering math. In fact, there was a time in our history when females were not expected to function well in math. therefore, it is urgent that we watch our words as we speak to each other. There are so many of our children who grow up in a negative environment and yet many use that "something" within themselves to prosper in spite of their environments and go far beyond the horrendous appearances to prove the greatness within themselves.

It is my personal belief that it is incumbent upon each of us to ponder and to query about that "something" within each of us... to acknowledge ourselves as being more powerful and effective beings than we previously thought we were. By doing so, we can live the kinds of lives we truly want to live that are more loving, healthy, joyful, and creative. I believe that we must learn this truth about ourselves and then help our children by teaching them (by modeling) about this awesome power that is within us that can help us and is always available to us.

By teaching our children about this inner power, we will help to create a generation of those who do not look outside of themselves and who no longer blame others for their successes or failures in life. But they will grow up aware of "something" within themselves which they can rely upon. They will not blame others if they have not attained the educational opportunities, career goals, and so forth. Some of us have already discovered this power within us, but there are so many others who don't know this truth yet. We no longer have to settle for our greater good. We have the power within us to come to that greater realization that we are, indeed, the captains of our own ships, and we don't have to give our ownership over to anyone or anything. With this kind of belief system, we can help to change our individual worlds and the world at large. I am reminded of the characters in a book I read many years ago entitled, *"Atlas Shrugged"* by Ayn Rand. It is really done unto us according to ...

"What You See... Is What You Get!"

Chapter 21

I AM

*Th*ese two words are so very important and yet so few of us realize this. We speak these words so indiscriminately without regard or awareness that we are creating a picture of either what we want or what we don't want to experience. "I am" is our true identity. When we say "I am" we are actually using an invisible and ever present power. If we were knowledgeable about our true identity – which is that invisible power that dwells in each and every one of us, we would certainly be more alert to what thoughts we attach to these two words, I Am.

To many, our corporeal selves and our physical existence are our reality. Actually though, there is an ever-present essence or energy that most of us don't truly believe in which is an invisible aspect of all persons and things that are visible. I think we all can agree that our thoughts are real –yet they are an invisible force. Have you ever contemplated just what you mean when you say, "I am"? Have you ever considered that whenever anyone says, "I am," those words are individualized in every instance? Let's say that Jennifer P. says, I am, She is referencing herself only and no other being. Even if Jennifer P. has an identical twin, the truth is that her I am is still uniquely her own self. Her I am refers to a wonderfully unique and unrepeatable being.

When we state I am and truly recognize that this is our true identity and that it defines who we think and believe we are, then possibly we will then make better choices with the adjectives that follow those two words.

Scientists who are engaged in the study of quantum physics discovered that every thought that we have carries some form of chemistry that transfers this energy onto our brains – which in turn, passes this energy onto our bodies. Then our bodies gather this information which manifests into our mental and physical well being or illness. So when we state I am healthy or otherwise, we are creating what will show up in our bodies as health or sickness. Therefore it seems that we have an innate ability to create healthy bodies for ourselves as we come to realize that when we think positive thoughts about who we are. We can state I am …(choose what you want to experience).

So when we say I am, let's be certain that we truly understand that we are using that invisible power that is within each of us. Just remember that …

"What You See... Is What You Get!"

Chapter 22

LOVE (OR APPRECIATION)

If we stop and consider the word *"love"* and the feelings that are attached to it, I am sure that we can't really get a handle on this word and sufficiently explain it to others' satisfaction. Yet we know and we sense that we can and do attach ourselves to others and even to things that we say are in the name of love. I have a painting on my wall, and whenever I look at it, I feel a sense of, "I really love this painting." A smile appears on my face, and a warm feeling emerges within me. I realized that those characteristics came from within me. Certainly they could not emanate from an inanimate object like a painting. From that realization, I know that there is an energy that is within me and all others that can cause even physiological changes in my body.

The effects of our love are certainly outer demonstrations of how we feel about ourselves, each other, inanimate objects, our pets and others. However, the cause behind those outer demonstrations of love are invisible and are a part of our beingness. If you dislike a person or thing, the same is true. The outer demonstrations of our feelings can be seen yet are not the cause—that is, the unseen or the invisible.

So, we can safely say that our emotions are born in an invisible place within us, but they are quite real to both the giver and the receiver. As you continue to live your life without accepting that there is an invisible aspect of us that directly impacts on the visible aspect of our lives, we will miss out on the realization that we are truly powerful beings who have absolute control over our lives. And that obviously is because that invisible component is the place that no one can touch, alter, or tamper with it in any way. Why? Because this is within you—an invisible "something." We have been taught that, it is done unto you as you believe. That is a reality whether we believe it or not.

If you'd care to test what I have shared with you, try this example: For at least one full week when you awaken in the morning say to yourself, "I am going to have a horrible day!" Keep this thought in mind as you prepare to go to work, school, or during any of your daily activities. As you interact with your family and friends, keep this thought in mind throughout the day. I can guarantee you that you are going to have a horrible day. Then, to be fully convinced, why not try the experiment again by starting your day off with the opposite thought: "I am going to have a wonderful day."

Why is there this correlation of our thoughts and feelings? It is because there is a power or presence within each of us that we can always use for our highest good. Unfortunately, too many of us either don't believe this, or we don't give any serious consideration to this possibility.

We are powerful beings, and I sometimes cringe when I hear people say, "I'm only human." I understand that this is what they ignorantly believe. But that is *not* the truth about us! Once we become aware of and accept this truth, we have begun a journey of self-discovery. And we have placed ourselves in a position to take charge of our lives and live positive and successful ones as well. However, the beginning of our spiritual quest to uncover our true identity comes from a place that we cannot point to and say, "Oh, yes, it's right here!" Yet it is real. We must be willing to relinquish our false belief or at least question the possibility of the reliability of this new thought that we are only physical beings. And just for the sake of curiosity, test and prove to ourselves that maybe -- just maybe it's true that ...

"What You See... Is What You Get!"

Chapter 23

RAISING THE WHITE FLAG

*W*hen soldiers are in combat fighting for their countries, there are times when they are forced to withdraw from the battle and surrender. In order to minimize further injuries and deaths to themselves, they raise a white flag to indicate to the other side that they give up. They have chosen to stop the fighting and just accept that the battle is over rather than needlessly fighting unto death. In essence, they are saying, "I surrender to your greater power."

In our individual lives, we may have had occasions in which we have had to give up our battle with some condition, situation, circumstance, or personality. And so, we have raised our metaphorical white flags by saying to our opponents, "Okay, okay. You're right." We let go of trying to convince others that we are right and they are wrong. Essentially, we have surrendered.

And before the dust settles from the previous battle, there is another challenge facing us. We are battle weary. Due to this constant battling, there is something within us that is gently nudging us to give it all up. At this point in some people's lives, they may engage in the use of drugs, inappropriate sexual habits, or alcohol. Some even consider suicide.

Too many of us just don't know what to do or where to go. All we want is relief from the battlefield of life. We just want some peace of mind. We are not yet aware that there really is the presence of a power within us that is ever ready for our use. We are not yet aware that the assistance that is capable of causing us to be winners is closer than our hands and feet and even closer than the very air that we breathe. However, there's just one problem with acquiring this assistance, and that is that we must believe in the reality of this truth. And for too many of us, the invisibility of this power tends to be troublesome because we are so used to believing in what our five senses tell us. We are not accustomed to getting still; that is, committing to stilling our minds and our bodies and just listening for guidance that will see us through this and every problem. Giving less attention (thoughts) to the manifest world and making it perfectly okay to "just be" in the present silence; this is called "just being" or... meditation.

In the past, prior to my introduction to the metaphysical philosophy, teaching and practice, I would feel so battle worn with having to deal with all of my life problems, I began a deliberate search for some kind of mental relief. Feeling battle worn, like many others, I read numerous books. I talked to others who were certain that there is an inner power that they may call God, Jehovah, Atman, Spirit, Divine Presence, etc. They often times had a different name for this presence or power – yet saying the same thing -- so I made a conscious decision to find out more about this invisible entity. My thoughts were that If I got enough reliable information, then maybe I would give this invisible power a try. I surely didn't have anything to lose. If it didn't work for me or exist for me, I could always just pick up my old way of living and continuing with the old battles that I was sure would wait for my return.

So, at the end of one day, feeling total battle weary, I plopped down in the nearest chair and resignedly declare, "God, I need help. Tell me what to do. I just need some help here." This was my moment of holding up that white flag and surrendering to that "something" that I have learned is greater than all the warriors I have ever experienced.

So this is how I began the journey of "seeing"—understanding that, if I let go and let God (in other words, surrender) and let this presence do for me all that so many others say it can, maybe I will experience a more peaceful life. Maybe I will see this earthly journey in a different way. Maybe I might not have to fight as much as I have in the past. I have come to know that,

"What You See... Is What You Get!"

Chapter 24

MORE POWERFUL THAN
A SPEEDING BULLET

In 1938, the artist Joe Shuster and writer Jerry Siegal created the superhero character, "Superman" in the Action Comics book series. Some years later, the hero appeared on television and in movies. At the opening of the television show, the narrator would announce in a most ebullient tone, "Faster than a speeding bullet … more powerful than a locomotive!" He was describing the powers of the character, Superman. And would you believe that all of us have, in a sense, as spiritual beings, the same capacity to affect changes in ourselves and to assist others as well? The rationale for this is that we have been gifted with a resoundingly powerful tool. This is not a fantasy. This is not something that was given to some and not to others. We all have an equal amount of this tool… this gift. Although each has a leaning towards a particular area such as a particular talent such as music, dance, mathematics, language arts, teaching, etc. This tool is our awesome minds!

Unfortunately, most human beings either don't believe this or are totally ignorant of this fact. When we encounter those whom we consider to be a genius, we don't even recognize the genius in our own selves And this is something that happens far too often. We compare ourselves to them and give no credit to our own abilities. It is a tremendous gift that we all have access to, but again, most human beings have not learned to fully utilize this powerful instrument. The effective use of this tool is not limited to a certain aspect of the community such as: ministers, politicians, professors of elite colleges and universities, CEO's of major business organizations, and others. No! Even that person who makes his bed on a piece of cardboard on the sidewalk has the same powerful tool available to him. Once we realize the availability of this awesome gift, we can learn how to train our minds to accomplish whatever good we desire. If you care to do a little research, you will discover that this is absolutely true. All the major universities throughout the world support this idea.

In the traditional religions, we have been taught to keep our eyes on our enemies. In reality, the closest enemy that we have to contend with is the enemy that is within us. Although it is a real challenge, once we learn how to properly use this valuable gift we can proceed to combat and defeat this and all other seeming enemies. That enemy within us tells us that we are worthless, weak, and powerless. Because of the lies that we have believed about ourselves, we are often lost on the sea of life being tossed about like a leaf that has fallen from a tree. We falsely believe that everything that our five senses attest to is the absolute truth for us. Too often, because we are unaware of this valuable gift, as the poet Tennyson stated, "It is closer than breathing and nearer than our hands and feet."

No one needs to be blamed. All that we need to do is to take charge of our lives by letting go of the past. Challenge anyone or anything that tell us that we are incapable of achieving anything that we have a "gut level" desire. We must come to acknowledge that the only good that the past can provide for us is that we can honor it as a tool for learning. If we stop and consider what part did we play in an encounter that didn't go well. Admit our own liability and simply move forward with a deeper understanding of ourselves. Our best teachers are our experiences. We then become our own best cheerleaders even when others don't cheer for us. We have fallen within the realm of many false beliefs that don't serve us. And so the time has come to simply take responsibility for changing our lives by looking at ourselves and doing our own soul searching. I am sure you have heard this many, many times: "If they knew better, they would do better." And this understanding, I definitely try to live by. Don't expect others to fix you. But certainly don't waste your precious time blaming yourself either. Especially when others may seem to tear you down, this is most emphatically the time for you to take the responsibility to honor yourself and build yourself up according to your own perspective of your understanding of a power that indwells you and your own uniqueness, desires and capabilities. So it is emphatically important how or what you think about yourself. That is a job that only you can do. You are the "I Am" within yourself.

There's something wonderful about this universe. When we decide to change our lives and begin that inner search, the universe seems to step up in assisting us. But the reality is that, it has been there for us all the time. We just had to step up for ourselves and recognize who we are. It provides the outside teachers and everything else that we need at that time to accomplish our desired goals. It is a glorious revelation when we discover that we are not alone on this life journey and that there is indeed something that is available, ready, and capable of supporting us when we arrive at the point in our lives and say to ourselves, "I am not satisfied with the way my life is showing up"? "I am ready to make a change." Ultimately from this perspective, we will discover this power that is within us. It may not at first work at the rate of a speeding bullet, but with our commitment and with persistence and faith in ourselves, the change will come, and we will be able to live our lives – ones that are filled with more joy, peace and abundance. We will develop a mindset that knows that we have that power within us that no one can take away from us. It is a power that enables us to bring greater good to ourselves personally and to those with whom we interact.

That inner power is our minds. It's invisible -- yet invaluable! So, when we come to that point in our lives, we realize that we can indeed think and speak our good into existence, because we have begun to change our belief systems. And we will come to know that we are not alone; neither are we powerless to effect change in our lives. I am not saying that we will never have any more undesirable experiences in our lives but with our newly found discovery, we can approach any difficulty in life with a sense of, I am empowered to overcome any and all challenges in our lives. We may even remember that they are our teachers and actually say, "Thank you" This is how I respond to my "opportunities or challenges now! This is using our minds in a powerful way.

But we cannot know this truth unless and until we make a conscious decision to just try it. Like any other thing, the more we practice this, the better we become in using this tool -- our minds. So, we practice and continue to practice in every event in our lives. Just like a musician or any other professional, the more we practice, the more proficient we become. And the practice is never ending. As it is with any other talent, ultimately you may be amazed at the power that is closer than hands and feet and even closer than the very air that you breathe.

When a perceived problem shows up in your life, that is the perfect time to practice using this power. Stop! Remember to love yourself. You can use the most powerful denial there is: "No!" Then affirm that which you feel is your own truth, such as, "I am a powerful being. I deserve greater good, and I now accept nothing less than that which is for my highest good."

There are innumerable books, websites, organizations, and groups that can help you in changing your mind about your worthiness. Aren't you tired of struggling with life and all its events? If you answered, "Yes!", then decide to be a true friend to yourself and surrender all your struggles. Make a conscious decision to try a new way of living. Use this tool -- your powerful mind—and you will eventually discover that what I am saying is as true as night follows day.

However, you must come to accept this as your reality. You can't accept my word or the word of any other person. You must experience this yourself and truly realize that ...

"What You See... Is What You Get!"

Chapter 25

IT MATTERS NOT

$\mathcal{I}$ have come to know about an East Indian philosopher named Jiddu Krishnamurti. In one of his discussions with his followers, he was asked why he always seemed to be at peace. He responded by stating that he was always at peace because it matters not what happens. Some of us may have probably heard this response before, even though it may have been worded in a slightly different manner.

When I read this, it struck an inner chord, and it had real meaning for me. As I continued to ponder the guru's response, what I began to "see"—to understand—was that Krishnamurti believed that it really didn't matter to him what situations, conditions, and circumstances were occurring in his life. But what did matter was what he thought about these events. If he saw them as a power (something or someone who had the power to threaten his life) he might react in a different way in order to thwart that eventuality. However, if he saw a person or an event as nonthreatening, he would have no need to resist, fight, or ward off this actuality. He could be at peace.

In the scriptures, we are given the same message: we must not resist evil (Matthew 5:39). And when we recognize, accept, and acknowledge that there is really only one power and one presence, then when we are threatened by any events in our lives, we can remain at peace and trust that presence and power to help us in all things. This is a high level of faith for all of us, but we won't know this truth until we try it.

If we see other people and events as powers that can impact either good or evil upon us, then we will not be able to respond to them. If we see it as evil, we will react to it by becoming angry, fearful, and doubtful. But, for sure, these people and events have a power over us only because we have given them this power, and only because we believed that they have power over us.

The astronomer and physicist Galileo supported Copernicus's model that the earth revolved around the sun rather than the other way around, which most people at that time believed to be true. He was ostracized and declared a heretic by the Inquisition of the Catholic Church in 1632 at the age of sixty-eight. He was kept in house arrest for the rest of his life. In spite of these threats on his life, he refused to change his mind about the discovery, and now, centuries later, we know that the theory has been proven to be correct. Christopher Columbus stood on his truth also even though he, too, was ostracized when he declared to Queen Isabella that the earth was not flat. He obviously thought it didn't matter what others thought and was able to convince her to sponsor him on his first trip, to acquire the three ships—the *Nina*, the *Pinta*, and the *Santa Maria*, and a sufficient crew to journey to another part of the world.

Throughout history, falsely accused men and women didn't care that they were ridiculed and in some cases imprisoned for what they believed. It didn't matter because they were aware of some personal power within themselves. And so they exuded a strength, persistence, and determination, and they were empowered to accomplish their desired goals. In modern-day history, we have read about athletes, musicians, and many everyday people who were told that they could not achieve their higher good, but these people, from all walks of life, persevered and realized that it mattered not what others were saying to them or about them. And this is still going on. When Misty Copeland, the world's most renowned ballerina was told that she didn't have the right body shape, or that she had begun the study and practice of ballet too late in her life and there were some who even implied – if not directed stated -- that her skin was the wrong color. All that was said to and about her had no impact on her decision for she had determined that…"It matters not." She only wanted to achieve her goal of becoming a top ballerina. Today the world has been blessed with a beautiful ballerina of tremendous talent, grace, and skill. Misty Copeland and so many others like her realized that …

"What You See... Is What You Get!"

Chapter 26

FIGHTING THE SHADOWS

I know that, if I asked people if they had ever bothered to fight their own or anyone else's shadow, I would get some weird looks, and they would probably begin to wonder about my sanity. So I now silently question others when I see or hear that they are fighting with people or events in their lives. To me, the demons they are fighting are like shadows. We all know that shadows can appear only if there is a source. In other words, a shadow cannot exist on its own; its existence relies entirely upon its source.

When we encounter other personalities, circumstances, conditions, and situations that ultimately cause us to become angry, jealous, fearful, and other negative emotions, it is the same as if we are fighting with a shadow. That source or cause of the confusion is you, and what you are angry with is a shadow. That person or situation has no more power than the shadow of a tree has. Some of you may think that this is such an absurd statement, but in reality, this is the absolute truth. The source and only cause in our lives is ourselves. All of our life experiences are related to the way we think about them.

When I wanted to learn how to skate more proficiently on my rollerblades, I took a course at the Learning Annex in New York City. Although I knew how to skate, I had not learned how to execute turns on my blades. When I asked my instructor to help me, his response to me was, "When you want to make a turn, simply *think turn*." You must know that, at the time, I thought he was being facetious or at best sarcastic. But, as I and other members of the class skated away from him, he eventually instructed us to turn and skate back to him. As I remembered his earlier instructions to me about making a turn, I did just that. Without additional guidance, I thought the thought, and seemingly like magic, I executed a perfect turn. This is the power that each of us has within ourselves.

Some of you may say that my skating experience is entirely different from other kinds of more complicated challenges we face in our lives. Here is where I would disagree with you. I can share with you several life-threatening situations in my life, and I truly believe that my life was saved each time because of the manner in which I thought about what was happening at that particular moment.

So let me share just one of these situations. While I was living in Atlanta, I had a full-time job and a part-time job. One day, when I was driving on Route 285 to my part-time employment, in the attempt to slow my speed to make my exit, I hit the brakes, but the pedal simply went straight to the floor without slowing the vehicle. Frighteningly, my brakes had failed. This was during the evening rush hour, and everyone was driving at a hefty speed. I began talking to God—that inner presence within me. Out loud I said to this Presence that I didn't want to get hurt, and neither did I want anyone else to get hurt. I asked for guidance. I steered my car as well as I could and kept in communication with that Presence within me. I was able to make my exit. For over a year, the traffic light at that exit had always been red whenever I approached it. That time, though, the traffic light turned green just as I approached it. After I made a scary left hand turn off the highway, I thought about a place behind the building where I worked where there was always a pile of sawdust. My thought that if I could get there, I could plow my car into that pile of sawdust and then pull on my emergency brake. And that is exactly what I did. I sustained a little bit of a neck injury from the sudden and jerky stop, but overall, I was safe and sound and no one was hurt!

I honestly believe -- No! I know that, if I had become fearful and hysterical; if I had panicked, I would have experienced a very different outcome. My conversation with that Divine Presence within me was my savior. As I said earlier, I have experienced other life-threatening situations. I am certain that what I now call shadows are definitely not powers. These shadows are simply manifestations of my thoughts and feelings. Again, in the metaphysical philosophy and teaching – they are the evidence of what is termed our "Consciousness." The incidents, I feel, were determined by the way in which I responded to the situations. The occurrences – that is, the situations, conditions, circumstances, events and personalities in my life are but shadows, and I refuse to be frightened by shadows that appear in my life. I now try never to succumb to the shadows, since I know that as I can keep my mind clear and understand that I am not a defenseless and powerless being who is manipulated by persons, situations, and circumstances. I don't always remember this truth, but I remember it more times than not. I know that there is a presence within me that is all powerful and causes me to succeed and be joyful in my everyday life experiences, both large and small. But it is up to me to realize that shadows are all around me. And this is not only my truth, but since we are all one spiritually, it is also true for others as well. But the shadows are nothing unless I am deceived into believing otherwise. That power is within me—within each of us. We just must realize this truth and come to know that ...

"What You See... Is What You Get!"

Chapter 27

FORGIVENESS

$\mathscr{F}$orgiveness is something that I am sure that many don't understand. The act of forgiving someone is not for the sake of the person whom we think has done harm to us; rather, the act of forgiving is for our own peace of mind because it causes us to be more open to a greater sense of joy and love for ourselves and others. When we can forgive (and another way of saying this is "letting go and letting God") we have taken our power away from that person and have empowered ourselves. Our minds and, of course, our behavior are no longer fixed on that other person.

When we are unable or unwilling to forgive, our minds are so stuck on that other person that, when we see or think of him or her, or even hear his or her name, we become annoyed, frustrated, or angry. Or we experience some other negative and binding emotion that not only affects us psychologically but also affects us physiologically. Our heart rate accelerates, we begin to perspire, and our respiration become labored. These and possibly other symptoms show up within our mental, emotional, and physical environment. Given all of this, we can say we have unconsciously given our power away to that person. Unfortunately, then we are not free. So we, ourselves, have placed ourselves behind mental and emotional prison bars.

Interestingly enough, you are the only one who has the key that can unlock those prison doors so that you can walk freely from your self-imposed imprisonment. Due to ignorance (unknowingness) on your part, you believe that it is the other person who can free you. Often we seek an apology from that other person believing that this act on their part will bring us "closure"; that is, will free us from our prison. We probably believe that, until we get an apology, we will not be able to forgive and move on with our lives. And this may never happen!

In many cases, the other person may have forgotten the incident or may never have given the matter the same level of importance that you have. He or she may even be surprised that you are still holding onto the so-called problem with such intensity. It is important only to you. So you continue to suffer, waiting for something that may never occur. Now you may ask why your feelings and thoughts about this situation seem not be important or relevant.

And my response to that legitimate inquiry is that your thoughts and feelings are very important, and they do matter. But the issue here is that, because you are important and you do matter, what matters mostly is your peace of mind, your mental and physical health, your awareness of your worthiness. So, do not give your personal power away by waiting for someone to cause you to feel better. What a waste of your deservedness! (I didn't make a mistake in using this word. I have the power to create!) So, as I mentioned earlier, forgiveness is not for the other person. Forgiveness is for your own highest good.

How can you experience peace, which is the greatest gift for us all-- when that peace is contingent upon someone else's decision to grant that peace to you? When we look at it from this perspective, we can better understand and maybe even accept the reality of the song lyrics written by Jill Jackson and Sy Miller : "Let there be peace on earth, and let it begin with me." To attain that peace, we must come to the realization that the past cannot be changed. It can, though, be an awesome lesson that can serve us in our new and continuing self-growth. If you are unable or refuse to forgive another for what you perceive was an injustice you have, in essence, voluntarily (although subjectively) placed yourself in prison, and you will remain there until you are willing to give up the thought of allowing yourself to give others power over you. And the relationship between that unforgiven person and you is like that of an actual prisoner and his jailer. Remember: if you cannot see yourselves forgiving the other person, then for sure ...

"What You See... Is What You Get!"

Chapter 28

AN ATTITUDE OF GRATITUDE

*W*hen we continue to work with ourselves on those afore-mentioned issues which I've discussed here, we ultimately get to a place where we understand that there is something within each of us that is greater than what our five senses reveal. Have you ever noticed that, when you ask someone to give you something and they agree to comply with your request, even before you receive that something, you say, "Thank you"? And you commence to act as though you already have it. This is what practically all of us do. It is a common practice or mode of behavior. That is what we do on the physical realm of existence. Why do we say thank you prior to our receiving the expected good? Simply because we believe (our thoughts) that we have already received it. From this expectation, we begin to feel better because our problem has been solved. "Whew"!

So it is on the spiritual or invisible plane. If you are expecting or desiring the gift of love, peace of mind, joy, wealth, or health, that right and perfect job, or some other highest good, simply say, "Thank you!" to the universe and begin acting as though you have already received that desired gift. Believe that there is an invisible power that is within you and all around you that will manifest that good in your life -- that demonstrated good that will most likely solve your problems. Spiritually, we call that our grace, but we must understand that it is not the gift itself that is the resolution to the problem; rather, it is your attitude—(your thoughts, your belief system)—that is your savior. That manifested good may pass away through the use of it, loss or deterioration or whatever but it is your mind (your belief system) that is the mainstay of your continuing good. And where is your mind? It is within you – always right where you are. Therefore we must remember that ...

"What You See... Is What You Get!"

Chapter 29

LOVE IS A WONDERFUL THING

*I*n 1991, Michael Bolton released a single called "Love Is A Wonderful Thing" (written by Bolton and Andrew Goldmark). Many years prior to that another song entitled, "Love Is A Many Splendid Thing" was published (music by Sammy Fain and lyrics by Paul Webster). And I don't think that there is anyone who would disagree with the message in either of these two songs. For they are, indeed, the truth.

We all use the word *love* so frequently and, I believe, much too casually. I often wonder how many of us, if pressured, would be able to give a definition of that word. What does it really mean to love someone or something? Over the years, I have asked many people to give me their definition of that wonderful word. What do you mean when you say, "I love you"? I ultimately came to the following conclusion, and please know that, as time passes and more information is garnered and my own awareness changes, then that conclusion may, indeed, change as well. For, as we all know, life is not static but is ever changing. What I believed or understood to be true yesterday may not apply today as I grow in my personal understanding, so my personal belief on any issue may alter.

We love our pets; we love our homes; we love our clothing items; we love certain stores, foods and restaurants; we love our family members and friends; and most importantly we love ourselves. And the list goes on endlessly.

When we get married, we commit to loving each other "... until death do us part". When dating, we profess our love to our partners. However, as we all know, we love others only as long as we agree on those issues that are important to us. If we have not learned how to disagree with each other and still honor and respect those differences, those promises fall by the wayside, and those promises of everlasting love may turn to resentment or even hatred. This is certainly true in the areas of politics, religion, race, and other major and minor concerns in our lives.

So, what I have discerned is that, when we say "I love you," that is a conditional statement. In reality, what we are saying is, "I will love you as long as you meet my expectations and my needs."

Certainly there is nothing wrong with disagreeing with another person, but of course we must learn to respect others' points of view even when they are different from our own. Therefore, we absolutely must learn how to disagree and be okay with the opinions of others that are contrary to our own. Most of us believe, however, that a mother's love is the closest to what we call unconditional love. This love has no requirements attached to it. Mothers tend to love and support their children regardless of how they behave. Their children may be the naughtiest creatures on earth. They may become involved in the most heinous criminal acts of all -- yet mothers will stand by their sides regardless of any unacceptable behavior. This may even be the case for most fathers as well.

The thing about unconditional love is that it is wonderful. And most importantly, we -- the givers and the receivers both prosper from unconditional love. We become better beings.

But the most interesting thing is that, without a doubt, we must learn to love ourselves as well. In our relationships, we must learn not to expect perfection in ourselves or in others. We have to learn to forgive others as well as ourselves for the mis-steps we make in life. When we are loved, we blossom in mind and in body. Our affairs are positively impacted because of our states of mind.

But we must be willing to give this love before we can receive it. In fact, this is a spiritual law. In a commonsense way, we all know this, even though we may not recognize it as a spiritual law. Simply stated, this law is: "As I give, so shall I receive."

However, too many of us believe that this attitude makes us too vulnerable, and we don't want to be hurt by others. Some may even misunderstand and believe that offering unconditional love to others makes them weak and that makes it easy for others to take advantage of them.

But unconditional love is simply, I believe, a matter of accepting others without criticism and judgment. We love others unconditionally and with wisdom. I am not saying that we must accept or like everything that others say or do, but we must realize that we can actually look beyond their behavior and see them as greater and better than what our physical eyes reveal to us. We can work with ourselves, as mothers do, and recognize that we may not like a particular behavior, but we understand that the person is doing his or her best according to what he or she understands.

How can we responsibly help this person (and even ourselves)? I know that it seems unreasonable or even, to some, impossible -- yet it is possible! Over the years, I have been learning to respond to life situations in just this manner, and by doing so, I have received more of that same love and appreciation from others. Although I make sure that I never expect anything from others; I just make sure I'm in a place of consciousness that enables me to accept that which is positively offered to me. Why? Because that's the best anyone can do at that moment according to what he or she understands.

Those of us who may be at variance with different aspects of the world's population, and who look to the scriptures for guidance for our daily living we read, that we should love the Lord, Thy God with all our heart, your mind and with all our strength and second to this we must love our neighbor as ourselves. Can you imagine how different our world would be if we followed this advice? If even half of the world's population would follow these directives, it is my belief that we would create a world of harmony and peace in our towns and cities, our states, our countries, and ultimately in our world. Throughout this country and possibly the world, wherever there is a Unity Church, the closing song is: "Let There Be Peace On Earth" (written by Jill Jackson-Miller and Sy Miller). But what I realize is that we cannot have peace on earth until we can see ourselves loving, appreciating, and respecting others in spite of our differences in culture, religion, class, etc. We can create a totally new and wonderful living environment for all of us.

"What You See... Is What You Get!"

Chapter 30

CONCLUSION

So, to conclude this most interesting discussion with you, let me repeat what I said at the onset. I am not attempting to convince anyone that my belief system is the only right one. Yet I am aware that millions of people throughout the world share these same thoughts and beliefs. I have facilitated workshops, written articles, given lectures on this subject, and I have met so many people who confirmed that these words are true for them as well. We all need reminders of these truths because it is not always easy to align ourselves with this perspective on life. Indeed, most of us have not been taught these truisms.

We who are in alignment with this philosophy must make a commitment to ourselves; we must be willing to be persistent and consistent as we practice these principles of life. In fact, those of you who may be relatively new to this metaphysical perspective should not, for sure, take my words as the truth. If you want to realize what I am affirming here, daily practice is essential and this leads to your personal experiences which then becomes the truth for you. In fact, I would even suggest that you try to prove me wrong. For our experiences are our best teachers. So many people in the world look at the physical environment and believe that it is their reality. What if we began, within our own communities, to deliberately practice to love, respect and appreciate all of our neighbors. Little by little, I know we would create the kind of world that we all say we truly want. If we can "see" this possibility, we can certainly create a new way of living.

So, in love and absolute appreciation and joy to those of you who have stayed with me to the end, I simply say, "Thank you all!" And let's keep reminding ourselves and others who are desirous of living greater lives that we must think and speak about these truths, but most importantly, live by them every moment of every day.

So peace, love, and blessings to all. And, as Flip Wilson's character, Geraldine, always said …

"What You See... Is What You Get!"

SUGGESTED READINGS

The Pathway Of Roses: Christian W. Larsen

Living The Infinite Way : Joel S. Goldsmith

Realization of Oneness : Joel Goldsmith

Within You Is The Power : Henry Thomas Hamlin

Thoughts Are Things : Ernest Holmes & Willis Kinnear

Wherever You Go – There You Are by: Jon Kabat-Zinn

The Hidden Side of Things : C W. Leadbeater

All Things Are Possible To Them That Believe : Annie Rix Militz

Collection: 7 Books : Annie Rix Militz

The Surrender Experiment: Michael Singer

The Untethered Soul : Michael Singer

ABOUT THE AUTHOR

Certifications & Experiences

- Ordained Minister, Universal Center for Truth
- Practitioner for Religious Science
- Ordained Minister, Ind. R.S. Church, NYC
- Guest Monthly Speaker, Beacon of Light Church, Santurce, PR
- Guest Speaker, Religious Science Church, Atlanta, GA
- Spiritual Leader, Center for Religious Science, NYC
- Writer of numerous spiritual articles
- Poetry writer
- Spiritual Counselor

At a time in Portia's life there were two words 1) religion and 2) church that had been banished from her world of consideration. She had become disenchanted and disappointed with those who professed themselves to be "Christians". Although she was actually afraid to call herself an atheist, she decided to compromise by calling herself an agnostic.

One day in 1978, she was invited, or maybe coerced is a better word to use, to attend a church service that had a different approach to religion and God. She later learned that this approach was called "metaphysics" and the church was affiliated with an organization called the Unity Church. On that day, although she didn't recognize it at that time, the rest of her life was literally changed. As the minister spoke on that day, she sat straight up on the church pew because it seemed to be speaking directly to and for her. After service Portia rushed to the bookstore and purchased a book by a well-known author named Catherine Ponder. On the first page of that book the words spoke to her and they were: "There's gold dust in the air and you deserve to have your share." The next Sunday, she joined that church. For five years, she never missed a single Sunday service. She attended as many workshops as she possibly could and took every class that was offered. Portia wanted to know everything about this teaching called "metaphysics". For her, this non-traditional approach to understanding her relationship with God – the Universe – made a lot of sense to her. It agreed with her soul. She wanted to learn more and more. And as she continued to study and practice the principles of this teaching; her life took turns that even she could not have imagined. For all those years, this teaching has proven its worth to her. At some of the most devastating moments in her life, what she learned has been her salvation at every turn. She has been blessed with phenomenal mentors to assist her in wading through the quagmire of life's lessons and finding her way to peace.

So as you can see from her accomplishments over the years, Portia has a lot to say and she wants to share that with all who are willing to listen and take to heart those principles of the universe which have helped her and so many others that she has personally counselled; through her workshops, seminars, Sunday lectures, etc. She hopes to continue to broaden this desire to help so many others by sharing her life experiences through her greater understanding and acceptance of is awesome approach to life.

Printed in the United States
by Baker & Taylor Publisher Services

Printed in the United States
by Baker & Taylor Publisher Services